Burgess Sport Teaching Series

TEACHING SOFTBALL

N. Sue Whiddon
Linda T. Hall

University of Florida

Illustrated by Andrea Goldberg
University of Florida

Burgess Publishing Company
Minneapolis, Minnesota

Consulting Editor: Robert D. Clayton, Colorado State University

Editorial: Wayne Schotanus, Marta Reynolds, Elisabeth Sövik
Art: Joan Gordon, Adelaide Trettel
Production: Morris Lundin, Pat Barnes
Composition: Jeanette Baynes

Cover design: Adelaide Trettel

Burgess Publishing Company
7108 Ohms Lane
Minneapolis, Minnesota 55435

0   9   8   7   6   5   4   3   2

Contents

Acknowledgments

We wish to express our sincere appreciation to those who assisted us in this endeavor by providing materials, pictures, diagrams and professional counsel. This special note of thanks is extended to the following contributors:

Ms. Lewanne Fenty, All-American slow pitch softball player; Ms. Jean Fountain, assistant director, City of North Miami, Department of Parks and Recreation; Ms. Jan Hager, Dunnellon Middle School, Dunnellon, Florida; Ms. Sonia Hoover, Gainesville High School, Gainesville, Florida; Ms. Bobbie Knowles, Palm Beach Community College, Palm Beach, Florida; Ms. Suzi Robinson, Central Florida Community College, Ocala, Florida; and Ms. Karen Kohl, University of Florida, Gainesville.

1

Introduction

Teaching Softball provides a comprehensive approach to teaching the skills and strategies of slow and fast-pitch softball. It is designed to serve primarily as a reference for physical education students preparing to teach and/or coach, softball teachers and clinicians, recreational leaders directing softball activities, and coaches in organized competitive softball programs.

Many teachers and coaches lack adequate training and sufficient sources of information to assist their players in attaining maximal skill and enjoyment. Other instructors tend to perpetuate the theories and techniques which they have personally experienced in classes or competition. Frequently, novice teachers seek methodological assistance in conducting well-organized classes and alleviating attitudinal and safety problems. Similarly, experienced educators and coaches are constantly searching for new ideas and motivational devices. Recognizing the need for relevant organizational and instructional information, the authors formulated this guidebook to facilitate optimal player participation, skill, and enjoyment.

The text is organized into nine sections. Chapter 1 introduces the reader to the content and design of the text.

Material to assist the teacher and coach in planning softball facilities and selecting equipment, as well as suggestions for making and caring for equipment, are discussed in Chapter 2.

Included in Chapter 3 are numerous conditioning exercises and activities designed to promote strength, flexibility, endurance, speed, and power. Each exercise is classified according to the components of fitness it promotes and its suitability for class or competitive purposes.

Techniques of class organization that facilitate instruction are presented in Chapter 4. A sample circuit practice is furnished to illustrate efficient class management.

Chapter 5 presents the program, objectives, class projects, and techniques for teaching basic offensive and defensive skills and strategies to beginning-level players. Many of the suggested drills were tested in pilot programs and were found helpful in developing skills and creating more effective class sessions. Obviously time will not permit usage of all of the described drills within a particular unit of instruction. Instead, the instructor must choose the most appropriate activities from the variety offered.

Objectives, performance descriptions of skills, teaching tips, and projects appropriate for advanced level players are offered in Chapter 6. The drills and activities in this chapter require prerequisite skills due to their complexity.

Lead-up activities and variations of the official game which, because of their adaptability, have proven to be popular in school and recreational settings, are presented in Chapter 7.

Procedures for evaluating player knowledge and skill are given in Chapter 8. Designed to assist the teacher in objective class assessment, the chapter presents appropriate skill tests and suggests content for written evaluations for both levels of player experience.

The administrative and organizational responsibilities of a competent coach are described in Chapter 9. Suggestions are included for pre-season and during-season game procedures and motivational techniques. Also presented are a sample practice schedule and pre-game warm ups which may have psychological as well as physiological value for the players and the team.

Performance objectives for each experience level appear in the appropriate chapters. Throughout the text, drill diagrams are provided, when necessary, to clarify player movement and group organization. The symbols used in the diagrams are explained in the legend that appears below. There is a glossary of terms at the end of the book. The rule guides mentioned in the Annotated Bibliography would be useful supplements to *Teaching Softball*.

Diagram Symbols

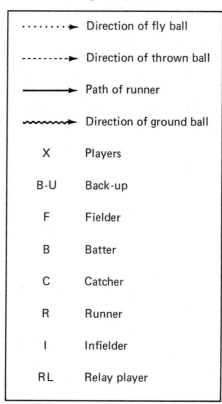

· · · · · · · ➤	Direction of fly ball
- - - - - - - ➤	Direction of thrown ball
⟶	Path of runner
∿∿∿∿➤	Direction of ground ball
X	Players
B-U	Back-up
F	Fielder
B	Batter
C	Catcher
R	Runner
I	Infielder
RL	Relay player

2

Facilities and Equipment

Physical educators and athletic coaches recognize the importance of desirable facilities and equipment in conducting safe and effective programs. Whether designing new facilities or modifying existing fields, teaching and coaching personnel should collaborate with architects and facility administrators. Likewise, teachers and coaches should have knowledge of the proper selection of equipment. Frequently, considerations such as cost, playing regulations, safety, and durability will dictate the type of equipment for a particular situation.

FACILITIES

Figure 2.1 illustrates the official dimensions and layout of a softball field. A softball diamond needs a smooth playing surface, a level outfield, and proper drainage. If space is available (a minimum of 4.65 acres), four softball fields are ideal for a school/recreational complex. Two fields, providing adequate space and facilitating supervision for a large physical education class, require a layout area of 2.32 acres. Fences are desirable, but not mandatory for school use.

Soil content should be tested prior to field construction. Large amounts of clay (over 15 percent) prevent proper drainage. A suggested mixture for playing fields is 75 percent soil, 15 percent silt, and 10 percent clay.[1] Fields should drain toward the foul lines with a 1 percent slope. The best grasses for general purpose fields are bluegrass and bermuda grass.

Ideal maintenance includes annual fertilizing of the grass, frequent repair of damaged areas on the field, installing built-in watering systems, and keeping turf about one and one-half to two inches high. Raking the soil smooths and levels the infield area and helps eliminate the hazards of the "bad bounce." This process generally requires expensive machinery. For proper maintenance, raking must be done regularly and also before each competitive event. Synthetic surfaces reduce maintenance and provide an attractive playing area. However, the synthetics have definite disadvantages. The hard, rug-like surface absorbs heat and causes sliding burns, sore legs, and difficulty in handling hard ground balls. It requires special shoes for play. Furthermore, the initial cost of laying the surface is a major inhibitor for most programs.

[1] Kenneth Penman, *Planning Physical Education and Athletic Facilities in Schools* (New York: John Wiley and Sons, 1977), p. 156.

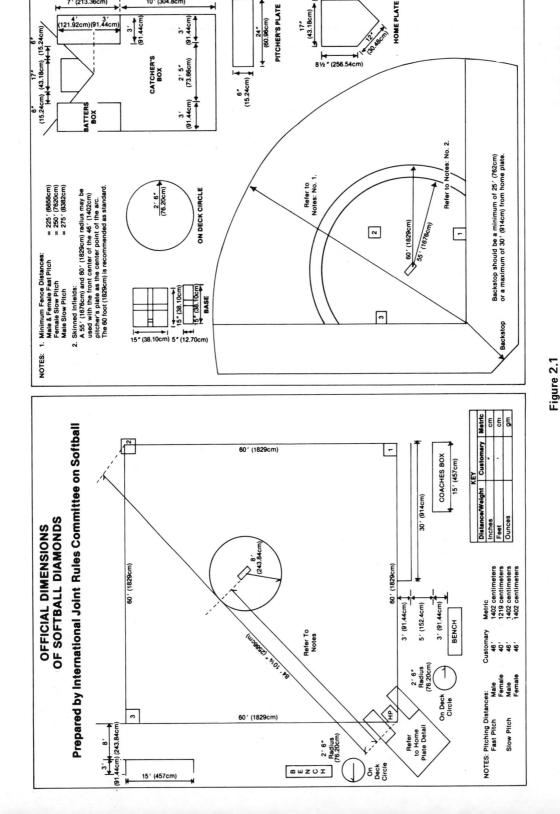

Figure 2.1

Official dimensions of a softball field. Reprinted from *N.A.G.W.S. Softball Guide, January, 1979* (Washington, D.C.: AAHPER, 1979).

Lines may be applied to the fields with paint or chalk. Plastic paint is durable and requires less effort to maintain. On the other hand chalk is cheaper, but requires relining, especially during frequent use of the playing field and after rainy weather. Also, it is desirable to freshly line fields before each official game.

Portable backstops and benches are frequently used to convert multipurpose fields into softball fields. Auxiliary facilities include scoreboards, batting cages, drinking fountains, bleachers, and lighting. Storage and maintenance provisions are desirable for competitive play, but not necessary for class use.

EQUIPMENT

In teaching situations, equipment of good quality should be purchased (Fig. 2.2). Considerations for purchasing equipment include accommodating right- and left-handed players, and providing equipment appropriate for the size of the participants. In coaching situations, players can have more choice in the selection of bats and gloves.

Purchasing the proper amount of equipment is important to any program and is frequently a problem for inexperienced teachers. A rule of thumb suggests that approximately one-fourth of the gloves and mitts ordered should be left-handed. The following ratio of items to the number of participants is recommended by the American Alliance for Health, Physical Education, Recreation and Dance[2] for class purposes:

Balls $\frac{1}{1}$	Mitts (first baseman's) $\frac{1}{10}$
Bases (set) $\frac{1}{20}$	Mitts (catcher's) $\frac{1}{10}$
Bats $\frac{1}{3}$	Protector $\frac{1}{20}$
Gloves $\frac{7}{20}$	Batting tees $\frac{1}{10}$
Mask $\frac{1}{20}$	

The official softball is a 12-inch ball weighing between six and one-fourth and seven ounces. It is composed of a kapok or cork core, wound with cotton, dipped in rubber cement and coated with horsehide. The exterior of the ball is smoothly seamed. When purchasing official balls, the buyer should be sure that all specifications are met. The Amateur Softball Association endorses certain manufacturers' brands, which conform to the association's high standards, and allows the ASA trademark to appear on the ball covers. Differences between brands are generally in size, seam construction, smoothness, and weights; all fall within the standards. Frequently official softballs with slight flaws in the leather are marked "seconds" by manufacturers and may be purchased at sizable discounts.

Generally, the regulation 12-inch ball is preferred for intermediate and advanced-players. However, official softballs may not be necessary or desirable for all class purposes. Elementary students may use the fleece balls or rubber playground balls. Twelve or 14-inch "super-soft" or restricted-flight balls are appropriate for teaching skills to young and inexperienced players. The softness decreases player fear in fielding batted balls, and permits balls to be caught easily with or without gloves.

The 16-inch ball is popular in secondary and college-level co-recreational leagues and co-education classes. Primarily used to offset differences in skill, the larger ball also allows advanced players to participate in limited space. One problem with using the larger balls, however, is that inexperienced players have difficulty throwing with sufficient power.

[2] American Alliance for Health, Physical Education, and Recreation, *Equipment and Supplies for Athletics, Physical Education and Recreation* (Washington, D.C.: AAHPER, 1960), p. 23.

Figure 2.2
Proper equipment is important.

Rubber-covered balls are suggested for damp playing surfaces, thus eliminating the possibility of water-saturated balls. Although quite durable, these balls are harder than those covered with leather.

Ideally, each player should have a properly fitting glove of good quality. The glove is an important teaching and learning aid, as it protects the hand and reduces the player's fear of injury. The school or recreation department should attempt to provide gloves for all players whenever feasible. If the department cannot afford to purchase gloves, players should be encouraged to bring their own. Whenever personal items are used in class, certain precautions should be taken to protect the equipment from loss or theft. Students should print their names with indelible ink inside their gloves. Personal equipment should be stored in personal lockers or checked in and out of the equipment room. Teachers may approach recreational teams, individuals, or business people in the community to obtain new or discarded gloves suitable for class use. Fund-raising projects may provide another means of obtaining equipment.

The official rules distinguish between glove and mitt construction. Mitts, gloves without separate fingers, are permitted for the catcher and first baseman only. The first baseman's mitt is more flexible and less padded than the catcher's mitt. For slow-pitch softball, catchers may use a regular glove. Before purchasing any gloves, several styles should be tested for pocket suitability and leather pliability.

In the interest of safety, the catcher should be required to wear a face mask and body protector during class play. Although not required by all official softball rules, this equipment is also recommended for recreational play and athletic competition. Certainly the wearing of a catcher's mask should be a minimal requirement for any player behind the plate.

In order to accommodate individual needs and preferences, a variety of bats should be available. Selections should include different weights and grip sizes. Bats may not exceed 34 inches in length and must have a safety grip. Most wooden bats are composed of northern white ash, while most metal bats are aluminum. Generally speaking, one bat for every five players will suffice for instructional purposes. Competitive teams may desire at least 20 bats to allow for breakage and to offer players a choice of weight and grip sizes. Players may also have preferences regarding the shape and style of the bat. Some bats are bottle shaped with the weight distribution close to the center; others are thin and tapered with the weight closer to the end. Shorter bats, with more mass in the hitting portion, are recommended for beginners. For liability and safety reasons, all bats should be checked daily for breaks, and discarded, not taped, if any breaks are discovered.

For competitive players desiring additional traction, shoes with metal or rubber cleats may be purchased in a variety of styles. Special rubber-cleated shoes are available for play on synthetic surfaces. Although the rubber cleats reduce the chance of injury to others, they do not offer the footing that the metal cleat provides. It should be noted that metal cleats may not be legal for high school competition and are not recommended for class play.

A competitive team should be outfitted in numbered uniforms of identical color and style which comply with league regulations. In addition, the governing association may require batting helmets for player protection.

Homemade Equipment

After purchasing the essential class or team equipment, the teacher or coach can reduce program costs by making other desirable items.

Ball and bat bags can be made by sewing together heavy pieces of canvas material and inserting a drawstring in a hem sewn across the top. Burlap or feed sacks sewn into one-and-a-half-foot squares and stuffed with sawdust make adequate bases when anchored to the ground. Resin bags can be similarly made by machine or hand.

Yarn wound into balls can be used by beginners for indoor skill practice and novelty games. Portable and permanent bat racks may be constructed for use on the playing field and in the equipment room.

A batting tee (Fig. 2.3) can be constructed from the following materials:[3]

1. One 1 × 12-inch base board, preferably with the end cut in the shape of home plate
2. One 1 × 10-inch top board about 10 inches in length
3. One pipe flange
4. One piece of 1¼-inch water pipe approximately 30-36 inches long with six holes drilled three inches apart starting at one end of the pipe
5. One piece of corded radiator hose, capable of sliding up and down over the water pipe
6. One nail
7. Four to six 1¼-inch screws

The steps in constructing the batting tee are:

1. Nail the flat top board to the center of the base board.
2. With screws, attach the pipe flange to the center of the top board.

[3] Margaret Dobson and Becky Sisley, *Softball for Girls* (New York: Ronald Press Co., 1971), pp. 13-15.

3. Screw the water pipe into the flange, with the holes at the bottom end of the pipe.
4. Slide the hose down over the top of the pipe, with the drilled holes exposed below the hose.
5. Insert the nail in one of the holes to act as a stopper for the hose. The selection of holes allows the batter to adjust the hose up and down the pipe to a preferred height.

Scoreboards may be as simple as a chalkboard, with innings marked off in paint and attachable number plates, or as elaborate as a lighted scoreboard. The former may be constructed easily and placed in a visible, out of bounds location along one sideline or in deep center field.

Care of Equipment

Gloves. Gloves may be cleaned with leather-cleaning products or with saddle soap and a small amount of water. To keep the leather supple and retain the desired shape of the glove, neatsfoot oil may be applied and a ball placed in the pocket. A string is wrapped around the glove tightly to support the ball in this position.

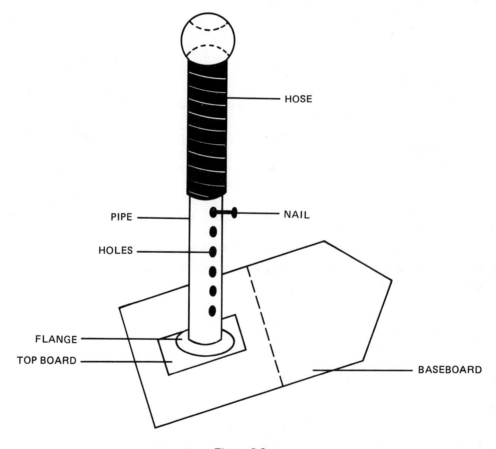

Figure 2.3
Batting tee. Adapted from Margaret Dobson and Becky Sisley, *Softball for Girls* (New York: Ronald Press Co., 1971).

Balls. Leather balls may be cleaned of mud, dirt, and grass stain by using saddle soap or a ball cleaner. Rubber-covered balls can be washed with soap and water.

Bats. Bats should be cleaned thoroughly following practices and games. A light oil should be applied periodically to prevent drying of wooden bats. Aluminum bats may be wiped off with a damp cloth and mild soap. Cracked or split bats should be discarded. No attempt should be made to repair broken bats. However, rough areas may be sanded and grips may be replaced. Bat handles must be checked for loose or unraveling tape. For storage, bats may be hung from bat racks or stored flat on shelves.

Shoes. When leather shoes are damp from wet playing surfaces, stuffing with paper and drying at room temperature maintains the shape. Oil applied to the leather tops and soles of the shoes helps prevent cracking. Canvas shoes can be washed with lukewarm water and soap. Laces and cleats should be checked before each practice and game and repaired if necessary. Insoles may be sprayed with disinfectant or powdered to prevent athlete's foot.

PROJECTS FOR THE PROSPECTIVE TEACHER/COACH

1. Visit a softball field and evaluate the condition of the facilities for safety.
2. With a partner, measure the various distances on a softball field to note its conformity to regulations.
3. Observe a maintenance crew preparing a field for play and explain in writing the technique employed.
4. Construct bat racks, ball bags, and batting tees.

3

Conditioning

Proper conditioning is a key element in preparing players to perform safely and efficiently. In addition, experienced teachers and coaches recognize the importance of warming up prior to a session of active drill participation. To aid in the physical development and bodily preparedness of a softball player, a conditioning program should stress the following components of fitness: strength, agility, flexibility, and endurance. The exercises presented in this chapter have been selected and organized according to these components. The simplicity and adaptability of the exercises make them suitable for a variety of programs and conditioning levels of the participants. Although an attempt has been made to designate suitability for class or competitive teams, certain exercises may be adaptable to both. Obviously, time will be a factor in determining the number of exercises to be included in each session. However, the instructor should attempt to encompass at least one exercise from each component group. In addition, *vita parcours* and obstacle courses may be designed to promote overall conditioning and challenge participants on all levels.

EXERCISES FOR CLASS INSTRUCTION

Strength

Pull-ups (arm and hand). Using an overhand grip, place both hands, shoulder width apart, on a horizontal bar. Raise the body until the chin is above the level of the bar. Lower the body to the starting position. Repeat three to five times.

Bent knee sit-ups (abdominal). Assume a bent knee position with hands placed on shoulders. Lower the body to the ground. Raise the body until the nose touches the knees. Do as many as possible in 60 seconds.

Modified push-ups (arms). From a hands and knees position, bend the arms and lower trunk to touch the chin to the ground. Raise back up to starting position. Repeat 25 times. Regulation push-ups may be used by assuming a prone position with weight distributed on hands and feet.

Agility

Shuttle run. Repeat two or three runs to a designated line, 60 feet from the starting line, and back to the start. *Option:* From a fielding position use a side shuffle step (slide) to alternate touches between the two lines. Repeat 50 times.

Footwork. Stand with feet shoulder-width apart, knees bent and body weight distributed on the balls of both feet. On the instructor's command move right, left, forward, or backward. Change direction as smoothly and quickly as possible.

Fielding warm-up drills. (Explained in chapters 5, 6, and 9.)

Flexibility

Straddle sit stretches. Sitting with legs in straddle position, touch head to left knee and sustain the stretch for approximately five seconds. Repeat the process, touching head to right knee. Perform three times to each side. *Option:* Use hurdle-sitting position to perform stretches.

Stride standing. From a standing position, bend trunk to right, left, forward, and backward, holding each position for five seconds.

Windmill. From a stride-standing position, twist trunk to the left and touch right hand to left foot. Return to starting position and twist trunk to the right until left hand touches right foot. Repeat this action five times to each side.

Foot to hand. Lie on back with arms extended out to sides at shoulder height. Lift right foot and touch to left hand. Keep shoulders and back flat on the ground. Return to starting position and touch left foot to right hand. Repeat five times to each side.

Endurance

Arm circles. With arms extended at sides and palms turned downward, rotate arms forward, making large circles 50 times. Turn palms upward and rotate extended arms backwards 50 times.

Bench step. Facing a bench 12-inches high, step up with right foot, left foot, then down with right foot and left foot respectively. Repeat for 60 seconds.

EXERCISES FOR COMPETITIVE TEAMS

Strength

Isometric rope pull (arms). Tie the end of a five-foot rope to a stationary object at approximately waist height. Tie the other end of the rope to the throwing hand. Sustain a pull against the rope for six seconds from the following positions: in the overarm throw, back, release point, and follow through. Repeat two more times, allowing for rest between effort.

Isometric squeeze (hand, wrist, forearm). Squeeze a tennis ball in each hand for eight seconds using maximum effort. Repeat three times.

Isometric bat drill (arms). Player assumes a batting stance. At backswing position, resistance is maintained on the bat in the opposite direction of the swing by a teammate. Both individuals maintain opposing pressure for eight seconds. Players rest for five seconds, and the bat is moved to the straight arm position and held at that spot for resistance. Proper wrist position must be maintained throughout the swing. This process is continued with the follow-through phase of the swing. Again, positions are held with resistance for eight seconds.

Isometric throw (arms). Player assumes a bent elbow throwing position. Partner places left hand under elbow of player (elbow at shoulder height) and right hand grasps player's wrist. Partner resists and the player holds a maximum contraction for ten seconds attempting to force hand forward and down.

Weight windup (hand, wrist, forearm). Attach a string supporting a five-pound weight to the center of a broom handle. Using an overhand grip, rotate the handle to wind string around it until the weight is raised to the top. Repeat a minimum of three times.

Agility

Lateral jump. Balance a dowel rod between two upright concrete blocks. Jump back and forth across the rod as many times as possible in 30 seconds.

Flexibility

Prior to team participation, the athlete should, slowly and smoothly, perform static stretching exercises. In each of the exercises the student reaches the maximum stretch position and holds that position for a designated time not exceeding one minute. Through these flexibility exercises, chances of injury are decreased and the muscles are prepared for the stress which will follow. Jerking and bobbing motions should be eliminated from the movement.

Wall exercise (leg flexibility and strength). Assume a position with back to a wall. With thigh parallel to the floor, move down the wall as if sitting in a chair. Hold this position to stretch the quadriceps.

Gastronemics exercise (leg). To stretch the gastronemics, assume a standing position facing a wall three feet away. Extend arms to wall to support body. With heels remaining flat on the floor and back straight, press body toward wall by bending the elbows. Hold at a 65-degree angle.

Shoulder stretching (shoulder). Assume a standing position with feet shoulder-width apart. The arms are extended straight in front of the body. With the fingers interlaced, raise the arms overhead while reversing the hand position. Force straight arms back as far as possible while the chin remains tucked. Hold this position, stretching the shoulders.

Endurance

Bleacher run. Taking one step at a time, players run up 15 rows of bleachers and back down. Repeat for 12 minutes.

Jump rope. Jump off both feet turning rope as rapidly as possible for 60 seconds.

Weight Training

Weight training uses a series of progressive-resistive exercises designed to develop strength and endurance. Exercises for the entire body, working through a full range of motion, should be included in a program. Both isotonic contraction (muscle fibers shorten) and eccentric contraction (muscle fibers lengthen) are involved in moving the weights. Isometric exercises (no shortening of muscle fibers) may be combined with a weight training program for rapid strength development. If isometrics are used, contractions should be held for eight seconds, with only one set per day recommended.

The duration of a weight training session should be 45 minutes to one hour in length. In setting up the program, each muscle group involved must be mechanically analyzed. Players should be pre-tested and retested periodically throughout the program to determine their maximum effort. The program should be utilized three times weekly while in pre-season training and twice a week during the season. All sessions should be preceded by a general warm-up. Records should be kept for each individual to assure proper progression.

For strength development, an overload principle is applied so the muscle is working against resistance greater than that to which it is accustomed. Weights should be heavy enough so that only four or five repetitions are possible. The last set for the workout should employ weights of maximum effort to allow only one or two repetitions.

For muscular-endurance development, the weight load for the initial set of an exercise should be heavy enough to allow only ten to 12 repetitions. The first three repetitions must be done smoothly and slowly to warm the muscle groups adequately. The second set weight load should allow only eight or nine repetitions. The final set uses weights which make more than seven repetitions impossible. An adequate interval between sets should be established.

Bench press (arm endurance and strength). Lie flat on bench or floor. Grasp barbell at straight-arm length above chest. Inhale deeply and lower barbell, *with control,* to chest. Do not pause when barbell reaches chest, but immediately exhale and raise barbell to original position. Keep feet flat on the floor and do not bridge back.

Calf raise (leg endurance and strength). Begin at standing position with barbell resting on back of shoulders. Rise on balls of feet and return to starting position. A block of wood under the balls of the feet increases the range of movement in the lower leg muscles.

Sit-ups (abdominal endurance and strength). Lie on an inclined plane with head at lower end, knees bent, and feet secured in place. Hold dumbbells on each shoulder throughout the exercise.

Barbell rowing (shoulder and arm endurance and strength). From a standing position, bend upper body forward until back is parallel to the floor. Flex knees slightly for comfort and balance. Grip barbell using an overhand grip, arms shoulder width apart. Lift barbell from floor and raise to chest, elbows close to body. Inhale when raising barbell from the floor and exhale when lowering it.

Leg bicep curls (leg endurance and strength). Lie face down on an inclined plane with head at upper end and weights on ankles. Inhale and flex legs until feet are close to hips. Exhale and slowly lower legs to starting position.

Dumbbell lateral raise (arm and chest endurance and strength). Start in bench press position, dumbbell in each hand facing one another. From this straight-arm position slowly lower dumbbells out to a position slightly below level of body. Inhale when lowering dumbbells and exhale when returing to starting position.

Behind the neck press (shoulder and arm endurance and strength). Grip barbell with wider grip than usual. Lift barbell from floor to resting position on shoulders. Inhale and press barbell until arms are extended overhead. Exhale and slowly lower barbell to position on shoulders. Do each repetition without resting.

Back extension (back and shoulder endurance and strength). Perform on high table or exercise bench. Lie on stomach with legs on bench and upper body over end of bench, hips forward. Partner holds legs. Grasp hands behind neck. Exhale and lower the upper body toward floor until body is in pike position. Inhale and raise upper body to position level with legs.

PROJECTS FOR THE PROSPECTIVE TEACHER/COACH

1. Observe a competitive team prior to the season and note the coach's conditioning ideas.
2. Talk with teachers and coaches concerning their opinions on the use of weights by their athletes prior to and during the season. Compare your findings with those of another student.
3. Talk with a professional or college varsity baseball or softball player on personal methods of conditioning.
4. Devise a circuit training program and chart daily progress for two to four weeks.

Class Organization

The goal of class organization is to structure the learning experiences so as to be meaningful to the students. Effective teachers and coaches realize the importance of good organization as it relates to safety, instruction, grouping, use of student leaders, and skill development. Factors which influence the organization of a class include the philosophy of the teacher, the objectives of the program, the number of leaders, the number of players, the size of the facilities, the availability of equipment, and the skill and interest level of the players.

SAFETY

When assuming liability for the welfare of students, the softball teacher must exercise forethought, good judgment, and adhere to sound safety practices. Good class organization helps to insure the safety of the players. Safety must be stressed in conditioning, warm-up activities, offensive and defensive techniques, and actual play. Policies should be made and strictly observed. The following are examples of safety procedures which might be employed:

1. In throwing and catching warm-up drills involving parallel lines:
    a. Adjacent players should be a safe distance from each other and equidistant from their partners.
    b. If the ball is missed, the player should retrieve the ball and return to the line before throwing it to the partner. This practice eliminates the hazards of making long inaccurate throws which might endanger unsuspecting players that are engaged in the drill.
    c. The first pair in the formation should take a position furthest from the equipment basket or instructional area, allowing subsequent partners to line up without walking behind or in front of those throwing.
2. Players should never throw the ball unless a target is made by the receiver. This procedure is discussed in Chapter 5.
3. Players should swing bats only when involved in a drill, or in areas designated by the leader. The designated swinging and batting areas are off-limits to all other players.
4. Specific areas should be assigned for teams and players waiting their turn at bat.
5. Injuries must be promptly reported to the instructor.
6. All equipment in need of repair must be reported to the instructor.

7. Players must be required to wear proper safety equipment.
8. After hitting the ball, the bat should be dropped—never slung or thrown.
9. When instruction is being given, players should hold the ball or put it on the ground.
10. Facilities should be properly maintained and be free from hazards that may cause injury.
11. Players should not be required to play when weather conditions are dangerous.

INSTRUCTIONAL TECHNIQUES

Poorly organized classes result in player apathy, which is frequently exemplified by a lack of motivation, "hustle," and attendance. The astute leader will give thoughtful attention to effective instructional techniques.

With respect to timing and sequence, there are several considerations to keep in mind. Verbal instruction should be succinct. Usually players are eager to participate and become restless when kept inactive for long periods of time. The presentation of information should be organized in a logical, progressive sequence. During each session, time should be allotted for instruction, drills, practice and play, if appropriate. Each session should focus on key points to be learned with time provided for players to learn a new skill or improve existing skills. New material should be presented early in the session while players are attentive. If suitable, the session should end with an enjoyable game in which the skills that have been learned are applied. The game may be a contest, a lead-up game, or a modified game.

Audio-visual Aids

Video tape or films allow students to see themselves in action. In addition to being an enjoyable activity, these viewings can also be valuable in pointing out the players' strengths and weaknesses. Other visual aids such as movies, loop films, and charts depicting skills or rules are useful in stimulating interest.

Use of Student Leaders

Student leaders can assist the teacher or coach in several ways. They can serve as peer teachers, role models for other students, or as officials, coaches, and statisticians. Additionally, they may monitor activities by directing drills, conducting warm-ups, and acting as station leaders in circuit training. Administratively, student leaders may assist in roll check, equipment accountability and facility inspection. Care must be taken to avoid exploitation of these valuable assistants. At no time should they be held responsible for conducting the class or practice, or assume a substitute teaching role. A leadership training program may be instituted to train students for these positions and develop their leadership skills.

Coping with the Environment

Conditions in the environment often influence the effectiveness of instruction. Factors such as other activities on the field, noise, temperature, wind, field condition, and position of the sun require special attention when instructing the group.

As a general rule the players should not look into the sun while receiving instruction. Sometimes, however, the sun may be less distracting to the players than facing activities which compete for their attention. Good voice projection is vital to being heard and to keeping the group's attention.

During instruction, players should be in front of and facing the leader. When possible, the instructor should enhance voice projection by not talking into the wind. A whistle may be used to signal a change of activities or to call the group together for instruction. When the whistle is blown, players should stop *all* activity and listen for directions. Indiscriminate or too frequent use of the whistle reduces the signal's effectiveness.

Throughout instruction, especially with the beginning groups, the leader should be mindful of left-handed players. It is often helpful to these players if the teacher, or a skilled left-handed student, is capable of demonstrating the movement or the entire skill with the left hand. However, if the leader is right-handed, this may be difficult. When possible, instructions should exclude the words "right" and "left." Instead, use descriptive terms such as "glove side," "throwing side," "front foot," "back foot." When using line formations for practicing a skill, such as swinging a bat, the left-handed players should be placed to the far right as the instructor views the line.

PRACTICE GROUP FORMATIONS

Dividing the group into squads is a commonly used technique for organizing players into manageable units for instruction. Another approach, squad formation, expedites and facilitates roll call, instruction, and drill practice. Generally, six players are assigned to a group for instruction and drills. Larger squads usually result in players having fewer opportunities for practice. For teams or drills requiring more players, squads may be combined. Several methods for classifying students into squads include: skill or motor tests, age or experience, physical fitness level, or student choice. Players may be homogeneously or heterogeneously grouped.

By grouping homogeneously, instruction can be directed to every player in that group since their abilities and their progression are basically the same. In addition, feelings of inadequacy within the groups are minimized as players are participating with those of similar ability. However, homogeneous grouping has some disadvantages. If groups are forced to compete against each other, the lower skilled groups may become discouraged. Also, the leadership within a particular group may be lacking.

Heterogeneous grouping also has advantages and disadvantages. One advantage is that the groups are approximately equal in ability, which facilitates game play. Heterogeneous grouping provides opportunities for the highly skilled to assist their less adept teammates. Social development is enhanced as students relate to others with different abilities. A disadvantage of heterogeneous grouping is that some students may be intimidated as the result of being placed in groups where other students are of superior ability. In addition, it is often difficult for the instructor to plan drills and practice sessions challenging to all players in heterogeneous groups.

One approach for consideration is to homogeneously group the class for skill development and heterogeneously group the class for game play. This allows the instructor to capitalize on the strengths of each method of grouping.

At times the leader may feel the purposes of the activity are best served by allowing the students to choose their own teams. When this is done, it is best for captains to meet with the teacher and select the groups in private. The players should not know the order in which they were chosen.

Leaders may determine that a less structured approach is appropriate, and instruct the students to count-off to form the groups. In this procedure, students line up and count-off in pairs or groups of threes, fours, fives, etc. (depending on the number of groups desired). If the leader is seeking heterogeneous grouping through this approach, care should be taken to see that students do not arrange themselves in line in order to get in the squad they desire.

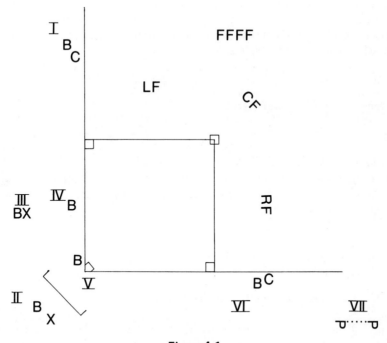

Figure 4.1
Circuit training organization

Circuit Training Organization

Circuit training, using a station-to-station approach, can assist the leader in keeping players actively engaged in various skill-developing activities. In teams or squads, the players rotate from station to station, practicing different skills at each station. In the following sample organization of a circuit practice, players are stationed as shown in the diagram (Fig. 4.1). After a specified time, players are signaled to rotate to the next station.

Station 1

Outfielders line up single file. A batter fungo hits balls to the fielders in the following manner: over player's head, to player's right, to player's left, in front of player, ground balls.

Station 2

With the batter six to eight feet from the backstop, a player to the side of the batter tosses balls which the batter hits into the backstop.

Station 3

See Isometric bat drill. The batter swings against resistance offered by another player.

Station 4

Batter assumes a position in foul territory between home and third. The batter takes mock practice swings as the pitched ball crosses the plate at Station Five.

Station 5

Batter hits ten pitched balls to infielders and outfielders.

Station 6

Balls are hit to outfielders from the batter at Station 5. Balls are fielded and thrown to second base. When the balls from Station 5 do not reach the outfield, the leader at Station 6, positioned on the first baseline, throws a ball to one of the outfielders. The outfielder fields the ball and throws to the catcher positioned beside the coach on first baseline.

Station 7

Pitchers practice pitching to each other.

PROJECTS FOR THE PROSPECTIVE TEACHER/COACH

1. Devise and list means for providing leadership opportunities for students during the instructional unit.
2. Develop a circuit training program to accommodate large classes.

5

Teaching Fundamental Skills

The purpose of this chapter is to present information that will aid in teaching novice players the fundamental skills of catching, throwing, batting, and baserunning. In determining the content appropriate for beginning players, the leader should give careful attention to each player's ability and attitude. Some players have limited experience or ability but great enthusiasm for softball; while other players may have had experiences which cause them to fear the game emotionally, physically, or both. The leader should try to avoid placing the beginning player in situations which might be frustrating or embarrassing. Provisions should be made for learning experiences that are meaningful and fun.

OBJECTIVES

For a unit of instruction to be meaningful, the teacher must have in mind particular goals and expectations for the student. Likewise, realistic objectives and a knowledge of how achievement will be determined may serve to motivate and direct the student. Performance objectives, commonly referred to as "behavioral objectives," are "specific statements of proposed educational outcomes."[1] The "specificity" refers to the three criteria which distinguish behavioral objectives from their more ambiguous counterparts. First, a behavioral objective must describe the exact performance, such as, "the student will be able to properly execute an overhand softball throw." Second, the minimum performance must be designated, such as, "the student will be able to properly execute an overhand softball throw a distance of 75 feet." Third, the behavioral objective must define how the performance will be evaluated, such as, "the student will be able to properly execute an overhand softball throw a distance of 75 feet at least once in three trials (AAHPERD Softball Skills Tests)." The explicit and unambiguous terminology, which characterizes behavioral objectives, gives the reader a clear understanding of the desired performances and their measurement.

In this chapter and Chapter 6, the suggested behavioral objectives will be classified according to Bloom's three domains of educational objectives: cognitive, psychomotor, and affective.[2]

The cognitive domain encompasses knowledge, comprehension, application, analysis, synthesis, and evaluation. In softball, the student must be able to apply these processes to learning the rules, techniques, and strategies of the game. Achievement of the objectives in this domain could be determined through observation of the student's performance in various game situations, or through discussion and written testing for understanding.

---

[1] Richard Cox, *Teaching Volleyball* (Minneapolis: Burgess Publishing Company, 1980), p. 2.
[2] *Ibid.*, pp. 3-5.

Objectives appropriate for the psychomotor domain involve specific motor and fitness skills. In a softball unit, the development of such skills as throwing, catching, batting, base running, and fielding are the "expected performances" of the psychomotor behavioral objectives. Acceptable evaluative techniques for this domain include observation, skill testing, and performance charting. Motivating students of various abilities to practice new skills and improve existing competencies is a challenge for any instructor.

Many teachers have difficulty in determining measurable performance objectives in the affective domain, which relate to feelings, attitudes, values and appreciations. Inherent to all instruction in physical education is the development of such desirable student qualities as leadership, sportsmanship, an improved self-image and value system, sensitivity to others, and adherance to the rules of play. In teaching a softball unit, the instructor may wish to promote positive attitudes and expressions through affective behavioral objectives. For example, students should be encouraged to demonstrate in game situations respect for the official's calls by accepting all decisions and addressing the official in a courteous manner. Once such objectives are determined for the group, participants should be encouraged to assist their peers in achieving the goals. Sensitivity to others, honesty, and the ability to be a team player are observable qualities which may carry over into other aspects of the student's life.

To enhance achievement in all three domains, the teacher should provide learning experiences which afford opportunities for development and individualized instruction. The text attempts to suggest some appropriate student activities in the form of drills, lead-up games, and projects which appear in this and subsequent chapters.

The objectives for this unit are listed as follows:

Cognitive Objectives

As a result of participating in this unit the student will:

1. Demonstrate a knowledge of the game and rules of softball by attaining a minimum grade of 70 percent on the written comprehensive examination for beginning level players.
2. Demonstrate through performance a knowledge of the duties and skills for each position on the field, and a basic understanding of the concept of team play.
3. Demonstrate cognitive knowledge of history, terminology and safety precautions through written reports, class discussions, and satisfactory performance by obtaining a minimum grade of 70 percent on the written examination.

Psychomotor Objectives

As a result of participating in this unit the student will:

1. Properly execute an underhand throw from a distance of 40 feet at moderate pace.
2. Properly execute an overhand throw from a distance of 90 feet (males) or 45 feet (females) which must reach the target baseman without bouncing.
3. Properly catch high, low, and ground balls thrown overhand from a distance of 50 feet as determined by the instructor's appraisal.
4. Bat a teed softball and a slowly pitched ball, using good form as determined by the instructor's appraisal.
5. Be able to meet minimum skill performance levels for the appropriate age group on each of the softball skill tests. (See Chapter 8.)

Affective Objectives

As a result of participation in this unit the student will:

1. Demonstrate an interest in the game by participating in practice and games during leisure time.
2. Demonstrate adherence to the rules of the game during competition.
3. Demonstrate positive interpersonal relationship by supporting and encouraging others.

DEFENSIVE SKILLS: CATCHING

When fielding, a player will have to catch thrown balls, ground balls, and fly balls. To catch hard-hit balls and balls hit to either side of, and away from, the fielder, the player must use additional skills which involve getting into the proper position. Beginners should be taught to effectively wear and use the glove.

Catching without a Glove

Learning to catch without a glove allows the beginner to better conceptualize the fundamentals of catching: watching the ball, relaxing the fingers, catching with both hands, and "giving" with the ball.

Performance Description

1. Watch the ball throughout its flight.
2. Position the hands and body in line with the path of the ball.
3. For balls chest high or higher, position the hands so the thumbs are close together and the fingers pointed upward (Fig. 5.1). For balls waist high and lower, position the hand with the little fingers close together and the fingers pointed downward (Fig. 5.2).
4. Extend the hands and arms toward the ball.
5. Open the hands and relax the fingers and arms.
6. Watch the ball come into the hands.
7. Absorb the force of the ball with both hands by giving with the hands, arms, and body.

Common Errors

1. Failure to relax the fingers and hands.
2. Closing the eyes or turning the head on impact.

Teaching Tips and Strategy

1. Softer and larger balls may be used when initially teaching catching.
2. Players should begin tossing and catching at close range.
3. The distance may be increased as players gain confidence.

Drills

To overcome fear in catching, the drills of "toss up" and "clap catch" may be used. From these self-paced drills the player may progress to throwing the ball against a wall, thus learning to judge the angle and speed of the ball.

Figure 5.1
Fingers upward

Figure 5.2
Fingers downward

Toss-up. Each player has a ball. The player tosses the ball into the air and catches it. The player should be encouraged to toss the ball as high as possible and still be able to catch it.

Clap catch. As players gain confidence in tossing the ball up in the air and catching it, a variation can be introduced in which the player claps the hands together one or more times while the ball is in the air. Players are encouraged to increase the number of claps by tossing the ball higher. Thus the player learns to judge the height of the ball and becomes accustomed to balls that are travelling a greater distance. If desired, players can compete to execute the most claps.

Catching with a Glove

Just prior to teaching the overhand throw, the proper use of the glove should be taught. The glove increases the likelihood of the ball being caught and reduces the chances of injury.

Performance Description

1. Place the fingers comfortably in the glove.
2. Watch the ball from the moment of the throw or hit.
3. Move quickly to a position in line with the flight of the ball.
4. Place the body and the glove in the proper position (Fig. 5.3). The glove position depends on the trajectory of the ball as described in catching without a glove.
5. Extend the hands and arms toward the ball.
6. Open the hands and glove. Relax the fingers.

Figure 5.3
Preparation for catch

Figure 5.4
"Giving" with the ball

7. Watch the ball come into the glove.
8. Catch with both hands.
9. Allow the hands and glove to fold or close around the ball.
10. "Give" with the ball with hands, arms, and body (Fig. 5.4).
11. Prepare to throw by bringing the ball to the throwing position.

Common Errors

1. Improper use of the glove. Closing the glove too soon.
2. Failure to catch with both hands.

Teaching Tips and Strategy

1. Confidence in catching fly balls may be developed by initially catching thrown balls from a short distance, and later increasing the distance and trajectory of the ball.
2. When teaching the correct method of using a glove, special emphasis should be given to opening the glove, allowing the ball to come into the glove, and closing the glove around the ball. "Let the glove do the work" is a good motto to adopt.
3. The glove should feel as though it is a natural part of the hand. This is best achieved by wearing the glove and catching with it as much as possible. Many teachers and coaches insist that players wear their gloves while they run laps or do footwork drills.
4. The presence of the glove does not reduce the importance of relaxing the fingers, catching with two hands, and giving with the ball. The use of the throwing hand aids in the catch and in preparation for a quick throw. As the ball enters the glove, the throwing hand traps the ball to keep it in the glove and initiate the throw.

5. Beginners often demonstrate a tendency to get the throwing hand in the way, or to try to catch the ball with the throwing hand. In order to avoid injury, these players should be given individualized attention and drilled on the proper mechanics.

6. In the early stages of learning, the target for the catch should be made by holding the glove at approximately shoulder height, slightly toward the throwing side of the body. This glove position causes fewer movements in preparation for the throw when the player is going to return the ball quickly. Also, the habit of throwing to a target helps insure that the ball is not thrown to someone who is not looking. "Do not throw the ball unless the fielder has made a target" should be constant warning to the players.

Drills

Since throwing and catching are practiced simultaneously, the drills listed for throwing practice are appropriate for both.

DEFENSIVE SKILLS: THROWING

The underhand and overhand throw are fundamental skills for beginners and should be taught in the early lessons of a unit. The underhand throw is used to pitch the ball to the batter or toss it gently to a nearby fielder. Beginning players should practice the skill of pitching as much as possible. The fun and excitement of the game is thwarted when the pitcher cannot get the ball over the plate for the batters to hit. Fielders use the overhand throw when throwing the ball long distances to other fielders or basemen.

Underhand Pitch and Throw

Introducing the underhand pitch or throw before teaching the overhand throw has several advantages.

1. It allows a longer practice time for a skill that often is insufficiently developed.
2. During the early practice and drill sessions it may help players overcome the fear of catching a ball that is thrown overhand.
3. The player achieves success with the underhand throw before becoming involved with the complex mechanics of the overhand throw.

Performance Description

1. Using a tripod or four-finger grip (Figs. 5.5, 5.6), hold the ball in front of the body.
2. Face the target. The foot on non-throwing side of the body is even with, or slightly behind, the foot on the throwing side of the body.
3. Bring the ball down and back in semicircular backswing. The arm straightens and the wrist cocks at the end of the backswing.
4. Step forward on the opposite foot and swing the arm forward in a pendular motion.
5. Snap the wrist, release the ball from the fingertips at the 8 o'clock position with a lifting motion.
6. Follow through (Fig. 5.7), step forward on the throwing-side foot, and assume the fielding position (Fig. 5.8).

Figure 5.5
Tripod grip

Figure 5.6
Four-finger grip

Figure 5.7
Follow through

Figure 5.8
Assume fielding position

Common Errors

1. Holding the ball on the palm of the hand.
2. Insufficient backswing.
3. Improper timing on release.
4. Lack of transfer of weight.
5. Insufficient follow through.
6. Failure to assume fielder's position.

Teaching Tips and Strategy

1. Initially, beginning players should stress accuracy in pitching the ball into the strike zone. Factors such as speed, arc, and spin should be introduced only after control is apparent.
2. The pitching skill may be practiced by having the players work in groups of three: a pitcher, a catcher, and batter. The batter does not attempt to bat the ball but assumes the batting stance. Having the batter present gives the pitcher a better perspective of the strike zone, and provides a better target area.
3. Although the underhand throw is the first stage in the development of throwing skills, the player should progress to the overhand throw as quickly as possible. Allowing the player to use the underhand throw exclusively for too long a period may deter or prolong the development of the overhand throw.
4. For safety and defensive reasons, strong emphasis must be placed on the pitcher assuming a balanced fielding position after the pitch.
5. The grip will vary according to the pitcher's hand size and ability to control the ball. The grip should be comfortable for the pitcher.
6. When using the underhand motion as a toss to a baseman who is in close range, the backswing is generally shorter and the ball is gently tossed to the player. (Fig. 5.9).
7. For both the underhand toss and pitch, emphasize a "lifting" motion and rolling the ball off the fingertips.
8. In slow pitch pitching, the pitcher should take several quick steps backward after the release of the ball. This puts the pitcher in a good fielding position in front of second base.

Figure 5.9
Underhand toss to a baseman

Drills

Target pitching. The pitcher practices by pitching the ball at the target on a wall or through a frame which designates the strike zone.

Slow pitch drill. Stretch a clothesline between two poles at a height of nine feet. From a distance of 46 feet, a pitcher practices arching the ball over the line to a catcher. *Option:* a backstop may be used instead of the clothesline.

Overhand Throw

The overhand throw may be described as a unilateral overarm motion in which the elbow swings forward ahead of the forearm and the forearm extends prior to the release.[1] The overhand throw is a basic skill for all positions. Proper development of the overhand throw allows the player to propel the ball with more velocity and accuracy than any other throw for distance.

Performance Description

1. Hold the ball in the fingers with a tripod grip or four-fingered grip.
2. Pivot on the throwing side foot, pointing the opposite hip, side and shoulder toward the target. At the same time bring the ball to a position above the shoulder at approximately ear height with the wrist cocked back. The upper arm is parallel to the ground and away from the body. (Fig. 5.10).
3. Step toward the target with the front (non-throwing) foot. Simultaneously, rotate the body toward the target in the following sequence: hips, trunk, shoulders.
4. Begin the forward swing of the arm by leading with the elbow.
5. With a snap of the wrist, release the ball from the finger tips. (Fig. 5.11).
6. Follow through toward the target, letting the arm come to rest near the hip on the non-throwing side.

Common Errors

1. Holding the ball in the palm of the hand.
2. Facing the target rather than pivoting.
3. Keeping the upper arm close to the body.
4. Failure to transfer the weight and rotate the body.
5. Failure to snap the wrist.
6. Failure to follow through.

[1] Ralph L. Wickstrom, *Fundamental Motor Patterns* (Philadelphia: Lea and Febiger, 1970), p. 71.

Figure 5.10
Pivot and back swing

Figure 5.11
Follow through

Teaching Tips and Strategy

1. Beginning players should start throwing and catching at a close range and gradually increase the distance and height of the throw.
2. Regardless of the distance the ball is thrown, the skill should be properly executed.
3. It is often helpful to compare the motion of the overhand throw to that of snapping a whip. Letting players actually "crack" a rope in a whip-like fashion may help them with this motion.
4. For long throws, players should take a couple of step-hops toward the target in preparation for the throw.

Drills

Two-player throw. Practicing proper fundamentals, two players face each other, form targets with gloves and throw.

Three-player throw. Three players form a line, with players on the ends facing the middle player (Fig. 5.12). Each player forms a target with the glove. Player number 1 throws the ball to player number 2. Player number 2 pivots on the glove-side and throws to player number 3. Fielding grounders may be added by having player number 2 (the center player) toss ground balls to the two end players. The end players throw the ball back to the middle player.

Four-player throw. Four player throw is basically the same as *three-player throw* except one player is added (Fig. 5.13).

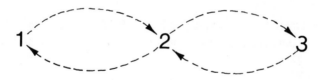

Figure 5.12
Three-player throw

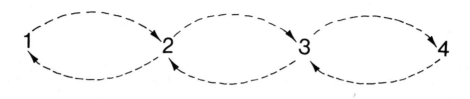

Figure 5.13
Four-player throw

Figure 5.14
Ready position

Figure 5.15
Fielding position

DEFENSIVE SKILLS: FIELDING

Fielding Ground Balls

Infielders and outfielders need constant practice in fielding ground balls. Practice should cover fielding balls to the right and left, requiring the players to use the slide and crossover steps.

Performance Description

1. Assume a ready position with the feet parallel, weight forward, knees and hips flexed and the hands close to the ground (Fig. 5.14).
2. As the ball is hit, move to a position in the path of the ball, keeping the body and glove low. If possible, move toward or "charge" the ball. If the ball is within two or three steps to either side of the fielder, a slide step is used. The slide step consists on a step-close-step, starting with the foot closest to the ball.
3. Once in line with the ball, bend the hips and knees in order to get the hands and body low to the ground (Fig. 5.15).
4. If the ball is several steps away, pivot on the foot closest to the ball, cross over with the opposite foot and move toward the ball.
5. Shift the body weight forward.
6. For routine ground balls, extend the arms toward the ball, and properly position the glove, touching the ground by the inside of the forward foot. Point the fingers to the ground. Field balls on the glove side of the body with the thumb away from the body (Fig. 5.16). Field balls on the non-glove side of the body with the glove in a backhand position (Fig. 5.17).
7. Keep the glove open, the head down and watch the ball enter the glove.
8. As the ball is caught, place the throwing hand over the ball and prepare for the throw.

Common Errors

1. Failure to get in the path of the ball.
2. Closing the eyes or turning or lifting the head prior to catching the ball.

Teaching Tips and Strategy

1. For the beginning players a ball softly thrown is less threatening than a batted ball.
2. Players should be reminded to keep the glove close to the ground and to use the body as a shield or wall in case the ball is mishandled.
3. For balls difficult to field, the outfielder may assume a position of one knee on the ground in order to block the ball. Blocking the ball is necessary in the following circumstances:
   a. When a single is hit to an outfielder and no one is on base, the fielder must not risk the ball getting by, thus allowing the runner to gain an extra base.
   b. When a passed ball would allow a runner to score, giving the team at bat the lead or the game.
4. Outfielders should receive many ground balls during practice. Hard ground balls hit from a short distance will aid the fielder in learning to judge and react to the ball.
5. To judge the speed or spin of the ball, fielders should watch the ball as it comes from the thrower's hand or leaves the bat.
6. "Playing the ball and not letting the ball play you" requires moving toward the ball in an aggressive manner.

Figure 5.16
Fielding on glove side

Figure 5.17
Fielding on non-glove side

Drills

   Chicken. Fielders stand facing each other about fifteen feet apart. Each player attempts to roll the ball between the feet of their partner by using quick, hard throws.

   Slide or cross-over step. The players are scattered approximately eight feet apart, facing a leader. Each player assumes a "ready position" to permit quick movement. On the commands "right-short" or "left-short," the group slides two steps to the right or the left when fielding a ball hit a short distance to the side of a player. Likewise, on the commands "far right" or "far left," the group uses the cross-over and three sliding steps to the right or left.

   Killers. Two players stand facing each other approximately twenty to twenty-five feet apart. One player tosses ground balls quickly in a mixture of right and left directions to the other player to force the fielder to stretch to field the ball. The players change roles after ten ground balls. The drill is more challenging if the thrower works with two balls at the same time. This causes the fielder to react more rapidly and provides conditioning for the legs.

   Pick-up. Two players face each other. One player throws grounders to the other's right, left, or front. Ideally, players should field the tosses without moving their feet.

   Catching ground balls. All players assume a double line formation with partners approximately 30 feet apart. One partner throws bouncing balls to the other partner. Before each grounder is thrown, the fielder assumes a "ready position." In order to insure getting the glove down low, the fielder must touch the ground with the glove before catching the oncoming ball. The player fields the ball as quickly as possible and throws the ball back to the first player. After 20 consecutive grounders, players change roles.

   Two-line grounders. Two shuttle lines of four or five players face each other (Fig. 5.18). The first player in line number 1 rolls the ball to the first player in line number 2. Player 1 then runs past player number 2's left shoulder while advancing to the end of number 2's line. Player number 2 moves forward to meet the ball, fields it and immediately rolls the ball to the next player in line number 1. The drill continues at a rapid pace with everyone moving. Another ball may be added in order to make the drill more challenging.

   Four-line grounders. All players line up according to the diagram (Fig. 5.19). The first player in line number 1 rolls the ball to the first player in line number 2 and goes to the end of that line. The first player in line number 2 fields the ball, rolls it to the first player in line number 3 and then

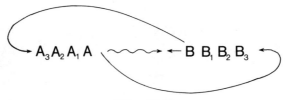

Figure 5.18
Two-line grounders

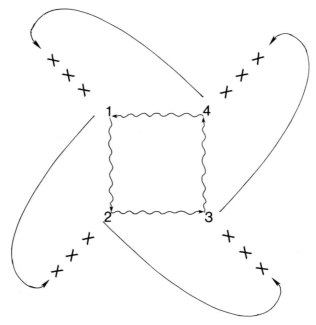

Figure 5.19
Four-line grounders

proceeds to the end of that line. The sequence continues with the first player in the line receiving the ball, then rolling to the first player in the opposite line and going to the end of that line. As the skill level advances, an additional ball may be added.

Around the world. Players line up one behind the other at position number 5 (Fig. 5.20). Upon successfully fielding a ground ball, the player moves to position number 4 and so on. Upon committing an error, the player remains at that position until all other players have had their turn. A chance factor may be added. After making an error, a player may chance it to be granted another opportunity at that position. Upon committing a second error, the fielding turn is completed and the player returns to position number 5. The object of the drill is to successfully advance through all positions before the other players.

Shuttle line infield practice. With a fungo hitter, players assume all infield positions except pitching. A series of balls, which include a slow grounder, a hard grounder, and balls to the right and left, are hit alternately to each position. Upon fielding each ball the player throws to first base. After fielding the series of balls, each player rotates clockwise to the next position. This drill may also be used for double play practice.

X

X

X

X

5   4   3   2   1

B

Figure 5.20
Around the world

Color throw. Infielders line up in a shuttle line formation at shortstop. Eight balls of four different colors are used for this drill (two yellow, two blue, two green, and two red). The batter randomly selects a ball and hits a grounder to the infielder. The player fields the ball and makes the throw to the appropriate base designated by the color of the ball: yellow, first base; blue, second base; green, third base; red, home.

Fielding hard-hit ground balls. Outfielders line up one behind another, just behind the base path facing the batter. The batter hits a hard ground ball to the first person in the line, who properly fields the ball, throws it to the catcher, and retreats to the end of the line. Ground balls should be hit alternately to the right, left, and directly to the fielder.

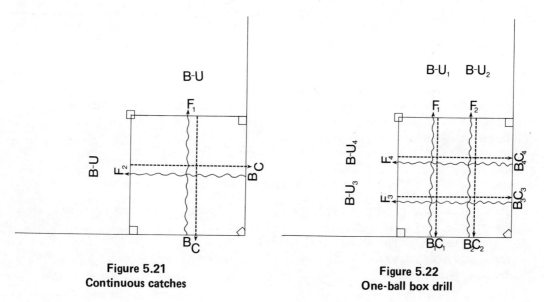

Figure 5.21
Continuous catches

Figure 5.22
One-ball box drill

Continuous catches (Fig. 5.21). Fielder number 1 takes a position halfway between first and second base behind the base path. Fielder number 2 takes a similar position halfway between second and third. Back-up fielders are positioned behind fielders number 1 and 2. A batter and catcher take a position opposite each fielder, and the batter fungo hits ground balls to the fielder. Fielders return the balls to their respective catchers. The batter continues hitting to the fielder until an error is made. As skill improves, the ground balls should be hit so they are more difficult to field.

One-ball box drill (Fig. 5.22). Sixteen players are involved in this drill: four batters, four catchers, four fielders, and four back-up players. The batters are placed along the foul lines between home and third, and home and first; two to each side. Each batter has a catcher. Batters along the first base line hit grounders to the shortstop and the third baseman. Respectively, batters on the third base line hit grounders to the first and second basemen. Each fielder fields the ball and returns it to the batter's catcher. Back-up players retrieve balls missed by fielders. Players rotate within groups on a signal. To avoid being hit by another ball, fielders should not cross the base line to field the ball. *Option:* Initially, fielders may roll the ball back to the catcher.

Two-ball box drill. This drill is the same as the *one-ball box drill* except the batter hits a second ball as the fielder throws the first ball to the catcher. All players must remain alert in this drill.

Fielding Fly Balls

Often beginners need special help and practice when learning to judge, and get into position for, easy pop-fly balls and balls hit in front, behind, and to the right and left of the body.

Performance Description

1. Assume a ready position with the hips and knees bent, the feet spread and the weight evenly distributed on the balls of the feet.
2. Move to a position in line with and under the ball as soon as the ball is hit.
3. Use a cross-over step when moving to field balls to the right or left of the body. When retreating in a backward right direction, pivot on the right foot, view the ball over the left shoulder and run diagonally to a position for the catch.
4. Watch the ball.
5. Position the non-throwing side foot forward.
6. Attempt to catch the ball approximately shoulder high on the throwing side of the body.
7. Catch with two hands.
8. Prepare for the throw.

Common Errors

1. Failure to be mentally alert, thus getting a late start on the ball.
2. Failure to adequately judge the ball, resulting in overrunning and allowing the ball to drop to the ground.
3. Preparing to throw before actually catching the ball.
4. Closing the glove too soon.
5. Improper glove position.

Teaching Tips and Strategy

1. Experience is the best method of learning to judge the flight of the ball and of moving into the proper position. Players frequently have difficulty judging the flight of line drives and "texas leaguers."
2. Players should run smoothly to the ball. A flat-footed run hinders judging the ball as it jars the eyes, head, and body.
3. Sunglasses or the glove may be used to shield the eyes from the sun.
4. Players should "call" for the ball in order to avoid confusion and collisions. Call out "mine," because the phrases "I've got it" or "I'll take it" may be confused with "You've got it" or "you take it." Generally, the first player to call for the ball should attempt the catch and the other player acknowledges by calling the fielder's name and moving behind the fielder.
5. When the ball is hit between outfielders, the player who can receive the ball on the glove side of the body calls for the ball and attempts the catch. The other player assumes a back up position.
6. Fielders should not be permitted to take more than one or two steps back peddling for deeply hit balls.
7. Generally, balls hit midway between the infield and outfield should be played by the outfielder as it is easier to run forward than backward and the forward momentum aids the throw after the catch. The outfielder should decide and signal who will make the catch.
8. Fielders should practice fielding pitched balls as well as balls that have been fungo hit.

Drills

Pop-fly drill. Infielders assume their normal positions. The batter fungo-hits pop flies near the pitcher's plate and home plate, offering the pitcher, catcher, and infielders opportunities for play. Each fielder calls for the ball prior to catching it.

Chasing fly balls. Fielders line up one behind another in left field. On signal, the first player runs at top speed toward center field. The coach throws or hits a ball which leads the fielder. After catching the ball, the fielder throws to the catcher and remains in center field until all players have moved in that direction. Fielders then practice chasing balls while moving toward left field. The coach continues to throw or hit balls until each player has made ten trips (five in each direction).

Changing directions. Players assume a scattered formation facing the leader. On the leader's command, players will run forward or backward, slide right or left, or turn and run backward-right or backward-left.

Sensational catches. The fielders line up in center field one behind the other and await their turns. A ball is thrown in front of, behind, to the right of, or to the left of each fielder at a distance that will force the fielder to catch the ball while running at top speed. The ball is quickly returned to the thrower.

Hits between infielders and outfielders. The batter hits short fly balls into areas between the infielders and outfielders. Players practice calling for each ball and outfielders will back the infielders in front of them. Outfielders must practice calling off infielders while moving toward the ball to make the catch.

Figure 5.23
Backing up

Backing Up

Performance Description

1. Get in line with the ball and assume a position of seven to ten feet behind the player fielding the ball (Fig. 5.23).
2. Avoid distracting the fielder.
3. Be prepared to catch any deflected balls or balls getting by the fielder.

Common Errors

1. Interfering with the fielder catching the ball.
2. Not hustling into back-up position as soon as the ball is hit.

Teaching Tips and Strategy

1. The outfielders have a responsibility to back-up on every play.
2. The left fielder backs up:
   a. The center fielder on balls hit to left-center field.
   b. Second base on throws from first and from the right fielder.
   c. The third baseman on balls hit to that position, rundowns or throws from the catcher, pitcher, first and second basemen, and the right and center fielders.
   d. The shortstop on all balls hit in that direction.
3. The center fielder backs up:
   a. The left and right fielder.
   b. Second base or balls hit to that position, rundowns and on throws from the catcher, pitcher, first and third basemen.
   c. The shortstop on all balls hit to that position.
4. The right fielder backs up:
   a. The center fielder on all balls hit to right-center field.

b. First base on all balls hit or thrown to that position.

c. Second base on throws from the third baseman, shortstop and left fielder and rundowns between second and third bases.

5. The shortstop backs up second and third bases on attempted steals and throws from the outfield, and the third baseman when fielding batted balls.

6. The second baseman's responsibilities include backing up second base when the shortstop is taking throws from the left fielder, pitcher, catcher, and the first baseman.

7. When a runner is not in scoring position, the catcher backs up first base.

8. The pitcher backs up throws to home and third base when runners are on base.

Covering

Performance Description

1. Know the responsibilities for covering a base in the various situations.

2. Move quickly to a position with one foot on the side of the base nearest the player fielding the ball.

3. Prepare to take the throw and execute the necessary play.

Teaching Tips and Strategy

1. The shortstop is responsible for covering second base when the ball is hit to the right of the field, and a play at second or a double play will be attempted. The shortstop also covers second on a double play attempt fielded by the first baseman. In this case the shortstop tags second base and relays the ball to first base covered by the second baseman. Third base must be covered when a runner is advancing to that base, and the third baseman is pulled away from the base to field a ball.

2. When the first baseman is pulled off the bag, the base may be covered by the pitcher or second baseman depending on the play. The shortstop covers second if the second baseman moves to first. On double play attempts when the ball is hit to the left side of the field, the second baseman covers second and relays the ball to first.

3. On overthrows or passed balls at home, the pitcher covers home plate.

Double Play

Performance Description

1. The basics of the double play involving the shortstop and second baseman consist of the following:

a. The player fielding the ball must know the speed and ability of the pivot person and time the throw so it reaches the bag at the same time as the pivot person.

2. The pivot person should:

a. Approach the base on a straight line with the throw.

b. Make a target with the glove about chin high.

c. Catch the ball with both hands as the bag is contacted with the non-throwing side foot.

d. Take another step after tagging the base, pivot on the throwing foot, and step toward first base.

e. Make the throw quickly and accurately with a snap or sidearm throw. (Fig. 5.24).

f. Get off the bag quickly to avoid collision with the advancing runner.

Figure 5.24
Double play

Common Errors

1. Improper timing in receiving the throw.
2. Not leaving the base after catching the ball in order to avoid an advancing baserunner.

Teaching Tips and Strategy

1. The pivot player should:
    a. Hustle to the base to receive the throw on arrival, as it is better to be early than late. The approach to the base should be in line with the oncoming throw and the bag.
    b. Do not throw to the next base if a play is not possible.
    c. Always be ready for a poor throw from the fielder.
    d. Be sure the foot is in contact with the bag when the ball is in the glove.
2. When the ball is fielded close to a base, the fielder should touch the base unassisted, and relay the throw.

Drills

Keystone combo. The coach alternates hitting ground balls to the second baseman and to the shortstop. The fielders take turns fielding, covering the bag, and throwing to first.
Double play practice. Batter is equipped with five or six balls.

1. A ground ball is fungo hit to the third baseman who throws to the second baseman who is covering second. The second baseman then relays the ball to first base.
2. A grounder is fungo hit to the shortstop, who throws to the second baseman covering the base. The second baseman then makes the relay to first.

3. The batter repeats the action to the right side of the infield, starting with the second baseman who throws to the shortstop covering second, and relays the ball to first.
4. A short ball is fungo hit in front of the plate to be fielded by the catcher, thrown to second, and relayed to first.

Turning two. The batter fungo hits grounders to various infielders. A player representing the batter runs to first base. Simultaneously a base runner on first attempts to reach second. Infielders attempt to successfully complete a double play.

Relay

The relay is a method of getting the ball from a deep outfield position to the infield by using two or three throws instead of one long throw. This technique offers the relayer options as to where to attempt a putout. On the other hand, if the ball is thrown a long distance from left field to home or third, the team forfeits its opportunity to make a play at another base. The relay is also a valuable tool when the outfielders lack the accuracy or strength to effectively throw the ball a long distance.

Performance Description

1. Go to a position slightly beyond the infield toward the outfielder fielding the ball.
2. Get in a direct line between the outfielder and the base to which the throw is to be made (Fig. 5.25).
3. Wave the arms to signal to the outfielder the direction of the throw.
4. Make a target with the glove on the non-throwing side.
5. Attempt to catch the ball on the non-throwing side, pivot and throw.

Common Errors

1. Failure to use the relay.
2. Not getting in direct line between the outfielder and the intended base.

Teaching Tips and Strategy

1. Depending on the situation, the first baseman, second baseman, or shortstop, acts as the relay player.
2. If the second baseman serves as the relay person, the shortstop verbally signals where the relayer should throw the ball and vice versa. Depending on the situation, verbal signals such as "third," "second," or "no play," should be given. Valuable time may be gained if the relay player knows where to throw the ball before catching it.

Drills

Outfield relay. Players line up according to the diagram (Fig. 5.26). The batter hits fly balls to the fielder. The fielder catches the ball and throws it to the relay player, who has moved into the proper position. The ball is then relayed to the catcher.

Deep hits and relay. Batter fungo hits deep fly balls to the outfielders who are stationed in normal positions. The shortstop goes into the outfield to relay all throws returned from left and left-center field. The second baseman acts as the relay for balls thrown from right and right-center field. The player not receiving the relay (second baseman or shortstop) should give the relay player directions as to where to throw the ball in the infield.

Figure 5.25
Relay

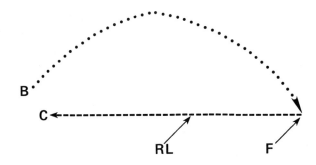

Figure 5.26
Outfield relay

Figure 5.27
Tagging a runner

Putting Out a Runner

Performance Description

1. If the runner is sliding into the base, assume a position straddling the base, and watch the ball until it is in the glove. Catch the ball with both hands, and lay the back of the gloved hand between the base and the runner's path (Fig. 5.27). After making the tag immediately move from the base.
2. In a force out, tag the base, and move immediately from the base.
3. When the tag is made off of the base, tag the runner with the ball in the glove.

Common Errors

1. Blocking the base without having possession of the ball.
2. Watching the approaching runner rather than the ball.
3. Failure to get out of the way after making the tag.

Teaching Tips and Strategy

1. Mishandled balls should be picked up with both hands. The eyes should be focused on the ball, not the runner. When hustling to make a play, the fielder should be sure that a play is possible before throwing.
2. Before each pitch the fielder should know the number of balls and strikes, the score, the position of the runners, and where the play should be made.

Drills

Tag out. The second baseman and shortstop assume normal positions with a runner halfway between first and second. The second baseman covering the base receives the throw from the catcher. The appropriate tag is made.

Force out. The second baseman and shortstop assume normal positions with a runner on first. The ball is hit to the second baseman who tosses to the shortstop who quickly moves off the base.

TIPS ON PLAYING DEFENSIVE POSITIONS
Infield (Fig. 5.28)

First Baseman

Attributes

1. A tall player, with good body extension, presents a target for the fielders making a throw.
2. A left-handed first baseman has an advantage in fielding bunts and throwing to other bases.
3. The first baseman must be able to catch high and low throws with one hand as well as two.

Responsibilities

1. The first baseman is responsible for covering the base on all plays and pickoff attempts at first, fielding bunts down the first base line, and relaying the ball from right field.

Techniques and Strategies

1. In fast pitch with no one on the base, the first baseman should play approximately five to six feet from the foul line and four to five feet in front of the baseline. For the same situation

in slow pitch, the baseman should be approximately eight to ten feet behind the baseline and eight feet toward second base.

2. In fast pitch with two strikes on the batter and the threat of bunting reduced, the first baseman should move to a position behind the baseline.

3. In fast pitch with a runner on first base, the baseman should assume a position approximately fifteen feet in front of the base, when anticipating a bunt.

4. As the ball is hit, the baseman should turn and move quickly to the base, face the thrower, and extend the glove or mitt forward about shoulder high as a target.

5. When stretching toward the throw, the foot on the glove or mitt side should be extended as far as possible toward the ball (Fig. 5.29). The other foot tags the inside of the bag and is quickly removed after the catch to avoid the runner.

6. On a pickoff attempt, the baseman should straddle the bag and make the glove tag low by the inside of the base.

7. For faulty throws it may be necessary to leave the base to make the catch. Once the ball is caught, the runner may be tagged.

Second Baseman

Attributes

1. The second baseman must be quick, agile, and adept at throwing from off-balanced positions after catching a ball.

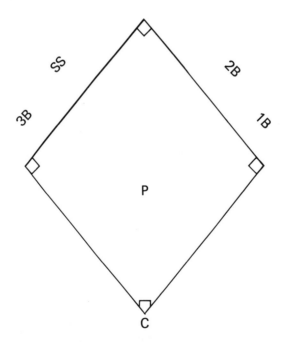

Figure 5.28
Infield positions

Figure 5.29
A first baseman stretches for a throw at first base

Responsibilities

1. The second baseman is responsible for covering the bag and pickoffs, and plays at second base on balls hit to the left side of field. In addition, the baseman may act as a relay for deep balls from right and center field.

Techniques and Strategies

1. The baseman's position is approximately 15 feet off the base and ten feet behind the baseline. This position varies according to the player's lateral fielding ability and if a runner is on first base. In the latter case, the baseman moves closer to second base.
2. When covering the base on close plays, the baseman should stretch toward the oncoming ball.
3. In covering second base on the forced double play, the baseman touches the bag with the right foot, steps to the inside of the base and pivots on the left foot to execute the relay to first.
4. With a runner on first, and a ground ball hit to the second baseman, a tag on the runner and a throw to first base should be the preferable play. If the runner attempts to avoid the tag by slowing down or running wide, the throw should be made to the shortstop covering second base. the throw should be made to the shortstop covering second base.

Shortstop

Attributes

1. The shortstop may be considered the key player in the infield due to the involvement in numerous plays and being in a position to direct play.
2. The position requires speed, a strong and accurate arm, and good lateral coverage.
3. The ability to charge balls, throw sidearm, cover second, relay ball from deep left field, and back up second and third bases instinctively are necessary attributes for the position.

Responsibilities

1. Cover second base on the double play when the throw is coming from the right side of the field.
2. Backing up the second baseman to throws to second from the catcher, pitcher, first baseman, right or center field.
3. Act as relay from left field.
4. Cover third base on bunted balls.
5. Back up third on fly balls to the outfield.

Techniques and Strategies

1. With no one on base, the shortstop assumes a position 20-25 feet from second base and 10 feet behind the baseline. With runners on base, the player may move in approximately four feet and slightly toward second.
2. In a double play situation, on balls hit to the shortstop's left and close to the bag, the player may make the play unassisted by touching second and relaying to first. If the shortstop is moving in a line other than toward second base when fielding, an underhand or snap throw may be appropriate.
3. When covering the initial base on a double play, the shortstop should catch the throw as the left foot touches the bag, step off the bag with the right foot and throw while stepping onto the left foot.

Third Baseman

Attributes

1. Playing the "hot corner" effectively requires courage, quick reactions, sure hands and a strong, accurate arm.

Responsibilities

1. The third baseman's responsibilities include fielding bunted balls down the baseline, catching shallow pop-ups in fair or foul territory, covering third base on steals, force plays, and pickoffs.

Techniques and Strategies

1. With no one on base, the third baseman plays three to four feet from the foul line and approximately even with or slightly behind the base.
2. With a runner on first and less than two outs, the baseman assumes a position three to four feet closer to home plate.
3. On slow hit balls toward shortstop, the baseman should move diagonally toward first and field the ball.
4. The third baseman may be in a better position than the pitcher and catcher for fielding a bunt down the third base line.
5. Proper positioning for a tag play includes straddling the base with the glove low. For a force out the base is touched with either foot and a step out of the base path is taken.

Catcher

Attributes

1. The catcher should possess leadership abilities and be able to work closely with the pitcher in determining the pitches to be thrown.
2. An agile and flexible catcher has an advantage in being able to come from a squatting to a throwing position quickly.
3. The catcher should develop a good overhand throw because of its strength and accuracy and it eliminates the possibility of hitting left-handed batters with the throw.
4. In fast pitch, a catcher with a strong arm and quick release discourages runners from stealing.
5. The catcher should be physically strong and able to put out runners charging home plate.
6. The catcher should be able to concentrate on catching the ball and not be distracted by the batter or baserunner.

Responsibilities

1. Making a signal for the pitcher.
2. Covering home plate.
3. Backing up first and third base.
4. Preventing a steal.
5. Fielding bunts and pop-ups around home plate.

Techniques and Strategies

1. The catcher squats with the weight evenly distributed on both feet which may be in a parallel or slightly forward stride position.
2. In fast pitch, a target is made with the mitt at shoulder height; in slow pitch the mitt is held on or near the ground slightly in front of the catcher.
3. The throwing hand should be protected by making a fist and placing it to the side of and in back of the mitt or glove.
4. When anticipating a steal, the catcher should go into a semi-squat position rather than a full squat.
5. Throws to a base should be made only when a putout is possible.
6. On a steal play with runners on first and third, hold the runner on third before attempting a throw to second.
7. When tagging a runner at home plate, assume a forward stride position in front of the plate facing the throw, catch the ball and turn toward the runner placing the glove low and in the base path so the runner's lead foot cannot touch the plate without being tagged.

Outfield (Figs. 5.30, 5.31, 5.32)

Attributes

1. Outfielders should have strong throwing arms, speed, and the ability to judge and catch fly balls.

Responsibilities

1. The responsibilities of an outfielder include backing up appropriate infielders, adjacent outfielders, and plays at the closest bases. Catching all balls within reach requires the outfielder to be alert and moving on every play.

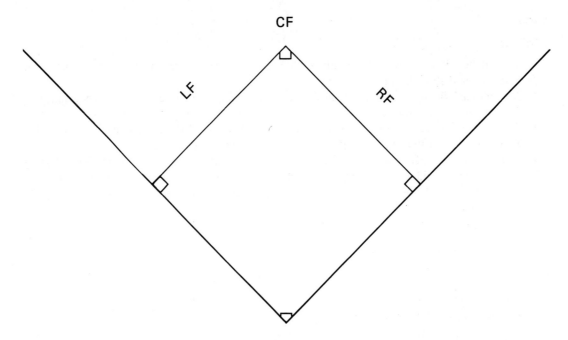

Figure 5.30
Fast pitch outfield positions

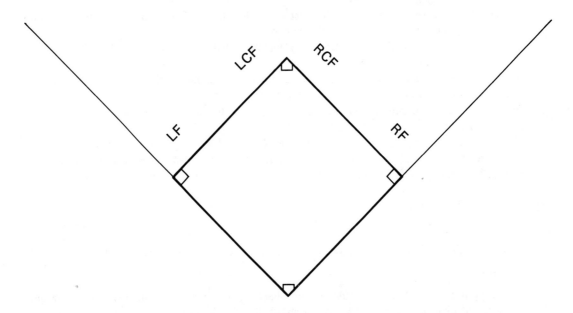

Figure 5.31
"Umbrella" slow pitch outfield positions

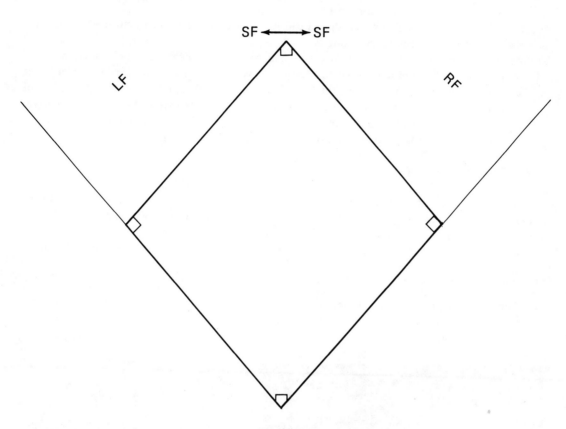

Figure 5.32
Short fielder slow pitch outfield positions

2. In fast pitch, the center fielder is the key outfielder with responsibility for covering the largest territory and backing up both adjacent fielders. In slow pitch, the center fielder's responsibilities are shared by the short or roving fielder.

Techniques and Strategies

1. On sharply hit balls to short right field with no one on base, or possibly a runner on first, the fielder may attempt a putout at first. Other fielders should throw to second base.
2. With one of the runners on third, after catching a fly ball the throw should be made to home plate. A fielded ground ball should be thrown into second or third.
3. On a long foul ball a runner on third may tag up and advance home after the catch. Therefore, the fielder should be in a position to make a throw to home plate.
4. Throws to home or third base should be kept low to save time, to allow a possible cutoff, and to assist the baseman in making the tag on a runner.

5. For each new batter, the outfielder assumes a position according to the ability of the batter and the game situation. This player must anticipate either a fly ball, grounder or line drive and know the appropriate action for each.
6. On balls hit between fielders, one should call for the ball and attempt to cut the ball off while the other assumes a back-up position.
7. As one fielder retrieves a deeply hit passed ball, the adjacent fielder assumes a relay position.
8. In slow pitch softball, a tenth player is designated as the short fielder or "roving fielder." The short fielder's position is between the infielders and outfielders, either to the right or left of second base depending on the strategy chosen for a particular batter. As a rover, the player assumes an outfielder's position in left-center or right-center field at a depth equal to the other outfielders. This formation is commonly referred to as "the fan" or the "umbrella."

OFFENSIVE SKILLS: BATTING

Being a successful batter involves more than simply hitting the ball. Players who understand the strategy of batting and who can capitalize on personal strengths will be a valuable asset to a team (Fig. 5.33). In addition to being able to hit the ball with power and accuracy, a good batter must also be able to study the pitcher, know when to take pitches, when to try for a walk, and which pitch to hit.

Performance Description

1. Grip the bat with the dominant hand above and adjacent to the non-dominant hand. Align the second joints of the top hand midway between the knuckles and second joints of the bottom hand (Fig. 5.34).

Figure 5.33
Lewanne Fenty, five-time All-American,
shows good batting form

Figure 5.34
Batting grip

Figure 5.35
Batting stance

2. Stand with the feet comfortably apart and the front of the body facing the plate. Bend the knees and evenly distribute the weight (Fig. 5.35).
3. Turn the head to look at the pitcher.
4. Bring the hands and bat to a position approximately shoulder high and slightly behind the back foot. The non-dominant arm is extended across the body and is held nearly parallel to the ground. The elbow of the dominant arm is bent and held away from the body. Cock the wrists and hold the bat in an upright or angular position. Watch the ball until it makes contact with the bat.
5. Begin the swing by striding toward the ball with the front foot. Sequentially rotate the hips, trunk, and shoulder toward the pitcher (Fig. 5.36). Extend the arms, snap the wrists and contact the ball in front of front hip (Fig. 5.37).
6. Follow through and drop the bat.

Common Errors

1. Separating the hands on the grip.
2. Assuming a stance in which the front of the body is turned toward the pitcher.
3. Holding the rear elbow close to the body.
4. Closing the eyes or lifting the head just prior to the hit.
5. Failure to transfer the weight.
6. Failure to follow through.
7. Swinging too early or too late.

Teaching Tips and Strategy

1. Players with poor eye-hand coordination often profit from hitting the ball from a batting tee. The batting tee allows the beginner to develop a complete, level swing without involving the problem of contacting a moving ball. In addition, it can be used to develop the basic swing. Emphasis should be placed on watching the ball and keeping the head down and stable throughout the swing. The tee should be positioned so the ball is contacted just in front of the forward hip.

Figure 5.36
Batting swing

Figure 5.37
Follow-through

2. The standard grip or "choke" grip is recommended for beginners.

3. Whether hitting a teed or pitched ball, choking up on the bat helps many batters have better control, thus they are more successful in making contact with the ball. The teacher should stress that the batter keep the butt end of the bat level during the swing. This helps to eliminate the problem of bruising the arms or stomach by hitting them with the butt of the bat. Frequently, this difficulty results from poor technique, using a bat that is too heavy, or both.

4. If players consistently hit grounders or pop-ups they should be reminded to execute a level follow through. Once the forward motion of the bat has begun, the hands should remain on a level plane below the shoulder.

5. Players should be taught to use a bat they can comfortably swing and keep under control. The first consideration in hitting should be controlling the bat and contacting the ball solidly. After control is achieved, the player should strive for power. Beginning players often have difficulty in hitting a pitched ball because of their eagerness to hit the ball hard. Drills should be used which will alleviate this problem and emphasize bat control.

6. Players often lift their heads before contact is made with the ball. Having the batter "look for the seams" or look for the color of a dot painted on the ball aids the player in watching the ball more effectively.

7. To correct an incomplete follow through, some teachers and coaches have found it helpful to place a towel or make a target area behind the batter's foot nearest the pitcher. The batter should complete the follow-through and drop the bat on the target. This habit also helps insure that the bat is not thrown in a dangerous manner.

8. Players should be instructed when to "hit away" or "take a pitch." For example, with three balls and one strike, the batter should hit the next pitch if it is in the strike zone. However, if the count is three balls and no strikes, the batter should not attempt to hit the next pitch. This situation forces the pitcher to throw a strike or relinquish a walk.

Drills

Batting tee. With fielders in normal positions the ball is placed on a batting tee. The batter then hits the stationary ball into the field. The batter is allowed a designated number of hits, then replaces a teammate in the field to allow each player to have a turn at bat. Emphasis should be placed on a level swing of the bat, keeping the eye on the ball, coordinating the swing with the shift in weight, and swinging through the ball. Another alternative is to use the batting tee while playing many of the suggested lead-up games.

Pepper. Four to six players line up side by side facing a batter 20 feet away (Fig. 5.38). The fielders pitch balls to the batter who hits grounders back to the fielders. Momentum may be added to the drill by using two balls.

Four-player pepper. Players line up according to the diagram (Fig. 5.39). The pitcher tosses to the batter. The batter hits the ball back to the pitcher. A backup player retrieves balls missed by the pitcher. A catcher retrieves balls missed by the batter. Positions are rotated after ten or 15 hits.

Hit and run. Each batter attempts to hit a designated number of pitched balls. On the final hit, the batter runs to first base at top speed.

Fungo hitting. Outfielders assume normal defensive positions. A batter fungo hits to alternate fields for place-hitting practice. Fielders return balls to the catcher. After ten successive hits all players rotate positions clockwise.

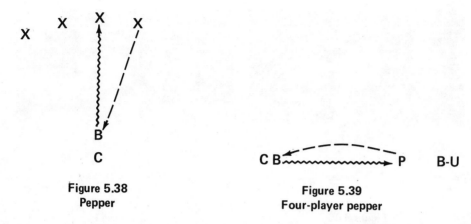

Figure 5.38
Pepper

Figure 5.39
Four-player pepper

Line ball. With six on a team, players face each other in two parallel lines 60 feet apart. Each team or side has a bat. A player on one team fungo hits a ground ball, attempting to drive the grounder through the other team's line of fielders. Team "B" likewise tries to bat the ball across the opponent's line. The bat is passed down the line so each player has an opportunity. As a safety precaution, be sure there is sufficient space between the players in the lines, only one team bats at a time, and the players call for the ball when fielding it.

OFFENSIVE SKILLS: BASERUNNING

Baserunning skills should not be overlooked in the early stages of overall skill development. Whether the game is won or lost is often determined by a team's baserunning skill and strategy. Techniques for leaving the batter's box, approaching the bases, rounding the base, and running from a base should be given attention in a beginning unit.

Running from the Batter's Box

Performance Description

1. After hitting the ball and dropping the bat, step toward first base with the rear foot (Fig. 5.40).
2. Advance toward first with the head up and the eyes focusing down the base path. Swing the arms freely, and push off with the balls of the feet.
3. On short pop-ups or any balls playable at first, run beyond first base at full speed.
4. If it is determined that an attempt should be made to continue to second base, swing outward five to six feet to the right of the base line approximately 15 feet before first base (Fig. 5.41). This manuever provides the best angle for continuing to second. Touch first base as the turn is made toward second.

Common Errors

1. Waiting to see if the ball is caught before running to first base.
2. Missing the base.
3. Stopping at first base rather than crossing it or rounding the bag.

Figure 5.40
Leaving batter's box

Figure 5.41
Swing out

Running from the Base

Performance Description

1. While waiting for the pitch, face the next base.
2. Place the left foot in a push-off position on the inside of the base.
3. Point the right foot toward the next base and shift the body weight forward (Fig. 5.42).
4. Allow the arms to hang freely.
5. Flex the knees and bend the torso forward.
6. Begin the run by pushing off with the back foot.

Figure 5.42
Push-off position

Figure 5.43
Touching inside corner

Common Errors

1. Watching the ball rather than focusing on the base.
2. Hesitating before sprinting.
3. Failure to listen to or watch for the base coach's signal.
4. Improperly rounding the base, resulting in a wide turn.
5. Missing the base.

Teaching Tips and Strategy

1. In slow-pitch the baserunner should leave the base when the ball crosses home plate or is hit. Fast pitch rules permit baserunners to lead off as the ball leaves the pitcher's hand.
2. Baserunners should attempt to take as many bases as possible on each hit without being overly risky.
3. With two outs all baserunners should advance as soon as the ball is hit.
4. When on third base with less than two outs, the runner should return to or stay on the base when fly balls are hit to the outfield. As the ball is caught, the coach signals the runner to sprint home.
5. A batter-baserunner advancing from home to first or from third to home should run in foul territory to avoid being hit by a batted or thrown ball.
6. Baserunners should run behind a player fielding a ball in the baseline to avoid interference or being tagged.
7. When a player is on second or third base and the ball is hit to an infielder, the runner should take a short leadoff and wait until the fielder throws to first before advancing.
8. The outward curve previously described for rounding first base is applied to each subsequent base when more than one base is attempted. The inside corner of the base may be touched with either foot as the runner pivots toward the next base (Fig. 5.43).
9. Upon approaching second, the baserunner looks to the third base coach for directions to take the turn or to stop at the base. The third base coach will also signal directions to runners approaching third.
10. To practice running beyond first base, draw a line 20 feet beyond the base, perpendicular to the baseline.

Drills

Take off. The baserunner starts at home plate. After a mock swing, the runner takes five to six powerful strides out of the batter's box with eyes focused on the first base coach. The player jogs the remaining distance to first base. As the runner rounds the base, five to six powerful strides toward second are taken. The runner continues this procedure at every base.

Base cornering. Players line up single file behind home plate. The first player runs at top speed to first base and makes a turn as if going to second. After making the turn, the player jogs back to home plate. One at a time each player repeats this action.

Sprints. Starting at home plate, the player runs three continuous sprints around the bases. After resting five seconds, two sprints are run. The player rests another five seconds and runs one final sprint.

Rabbit. Eight runners are placed as shown in the diagram (Fig. 5.44). On the signal "go" all players run and attempt to tag the player preceding them. Upon making a tag, the player who committed the tag may leave the drill. The tagged player must continue until tagging the preceding runner or the drill is discontinued.

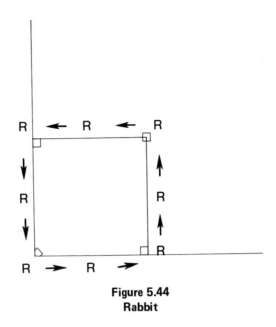

Figure 5.44
Rabbit

Designated Situations

The following game-like situations provide excellent practice for competition.

1. The batter hits a pitched ball to the infield and runs to first base. A baserunner may be placed beside the batter for the actual running.
2. The batter fungo hits a single to left field. The batter/baserunner touches first base and makes a turn toward second. If the ball is not fielded cleanly, the runner then advances to second.
3. With a runner on first, the batter fungo hits a single. The advancing baserunner looks at the third base coach just before touching second base, and either stops or continues as signaled.
4. With a runner on second base, a batter fungo hits a base hit. The runner on second attempts to score.
5. With a runner on second, the batter fungo hits a ball in front of the runner to the shortstop. The runner takes a lead, then advances as the throw is made to first base.
6. With a runner on second, a batter hits between the first and second baseman. The runner attempts to advance to third.

Sacrifice Fly

With less than two outs, a sacrifice fly may be used to advance a baserunner at the expense of the batter being put out. This technique is frequently used to score a runner or place a runner in scoring position.

Performance Description

1. The batter hits a long fly ball to the outfield.
2. The baserunner stays on the base in the takeoff position.
3. As the ball is caught or missed the baserunner sprints to the next base.

Common Errors

1. Inability of the batter to hit the ball to the outfield.
2. Failure of the baserunner to tag the base and leave immediately when the ball is caught.
3. Leaving the base before the ball is caught forcing a retreat to tag up before an advance is possible.
4. Failure of the baserunner to listen to the base coach.

Drills

1. The batter hits a long fly ball to the outfield, the baserunner "tags up" at the base. As the ball is caught or missed the baserunner runs to the next base.

Teaching Tips

1. When there are less than two outs, a sacrifice fly may be used to advance a baserunner at the expense of the batter being put out.
2. Often the baserunner will cause the fielder to hurry and make a throwing error by faking an advance for the next base. If an error is made and the situation warrants, the baserunner advances.

SAMPLE LESSON PLANS

This sample unit consists of 20 adaptable lesson plans. During each session new material should be discussed, demonstrated, and practiced in drills. In later sessions, game play will allow for the application of acquired skills. Appropriate conditioning and warm-up exercises should preempt participation. Rules, strategy, and terminology should be introduced when appropriate. Evaluation should be scheduled periodically throughout the unit.

Day 1 Psychomotor assessment
Day 2 a. Introduction to the game
       b. Introduction to catching
Day 3 a. Continue basic catching skills
       b. Introduce the underhand throw
         or pitch
       c. Play lead-up games
Day 4 a. Review skills
       b. Introduce the overhand throw
       c. Play lead-up game
Day 5 a. Review skills
       b. Introduce fielding ground balls
       c. Play lead-up games
Day 6 a. Review previous skills
       b. Introduce catching fly balls
Day 7 a. Introduce game rules: slow and
         fast pitch
       b. Play lead-up game: Throw Softball
Day 8 a. Review fielding skills
       b. Introduce batting from a tee

Day 9 a. Introduce hitting a pitched ball
       b. Play lead-up games
Day 10 a. Review skills by playing lead-up
         games: Team Pepper and Peggy
       b. Introduce baserunning
       c. Play lead-up games: Around the Horn
Day 11 a. Psychomotor assessment
Day 12 a. Quiz
       b. Review skills through selected drills
Day 13 a. Play regulation softball
Day 14 a. Play regulation softball
Day 15 a. Play modified game
Day 16 a. Tournament and psychomotor
         assessment
Day 17 a. Tournament and psychomotor
         assessment
Day 18 a. Tournament and psychomotor
         assessment
Day 19 a. Psychomotor assessment
Day 20 a. Written evaluation

PROJECTS FOR THE PROSPECTIVE TEACHER/LEADER

1. Design, record, and evaluate progress on a personal improvement chart for a player.
2. Teach a skill of choice to a beginning player.
3. Using an analysis chart, view a video tape of yourself in action.
4. Interview a teacher or recreation leader to determine problems in teaching a beginner.
5. Prepare a bulletin board showing slow and fast pitch positions.
6. Design three softball drills involving 10 players.

6

Teaching
Advanced Skills

The activities in this chapter are designed for players who can properly execute the fundamental skills, and possess an understanding of the basic terminology, rules, and strategy of the game. In advanced level play, a player must possess the ability to think quickly, charge the ball, throw on the run, bunt, and place hit.

Although new skills are introduced at this level, continuing emphasis should be placed on developing existing skills. The teacher must remember that advanced players often need to review fundamental skills and strategies to assure mastery of these techniques. Previously taught drills may be used as warm-ups for the practice sessions. The more complex drills introduced in this chapter frequently combine a new skill with existing fundamentals for additional learning reinforcement.

Mastery of the techniques and activities in this chapter should be a challenge to the advanced player. Quickness, accuracy, and excellence in every aspect of the game should be a meaningful theme for all practices. Furthermore, many of the suggested drills are designed to promote player concentration and preparedness through performance of skills in game-like situations.

OBJECTIVES

The objectives for this unit are presented as follows:*

Cognitive objectives. As a result of participation in this unit, the student will:
1. Demonstrate a thorough knowledge of the game and rules of softball by attaining a minimum grade of 70 percent on the written comprehensive examination for advanced level players.
2. Demonstrate conceptual knowledge of slow or fast-pitch strategy through written reports, class discussions, and satisfactory performance (70 percent efficiency) on the advanced level written examination.
3. Demonstrate an understanding of defensive play by diagramming positions and outlining responsibilities of each player in various situations.

* Refer to Chapter 5 for explanation of objectives.

Psychomotor objectives. As a result of participating in this softball unit, the student will:

1. Properly execute a strong overhand throw from a distance of 160 feet (male), 75 feet (female), which must reach the target without bouncing.
2. Properly execute the sidearm throw from a distance of 60 feet (male and female) as determined by the instructor's appraisal.
3. Catch balls batted to the side, front, and over the player's head from a distance of 50 feet. The student must use proper form in catching as determined by the instructor's appraisal.
4. Place hit balls to specific areas on the field when pitched at a rapid speed (fast pitch) or with a high arc and spin (slow pitch).
5. Apply proper technique and strategy to all baserunning situations, including sliding, as evidenced in game play.
6. Meet minimum skill performance levels for the appropriate age groups on each of the softball skill tests. (See Chapter 8)

Affective objectives. As a result of participating in this softball unit, the student will:

1. Demonstrate an appreciation and understanding of the role of the officials through exemplary respect for their decisions.
2. Express an interest and appreciation for the game through participation in extracurricular or community softball programs.
3. Indicate an appreciation for high caliber play by leisure time attendance or viewing of advanced level competition.

DEFENSIVE SKILLS: ADVANCED THROWING AND CATCHING

Advanced players must be able to catch hard-hit or thrown balls safely and without error. In improving their throwing techniques, players should strive for quick releases and accuracy. Hustling tactics, including charging shallow balls and throwing on the run, should be a part of each player's skill repertoire. Through challenging practices, which place increasing demands on the players, basic skills may be further developed. At this level, each player should be encouraged to increase personal expectations and develop self-motivation for improvement.

Performance Description

1. Emphasize "giving" with the ball when catching hard throws or batted balls by relaxing and recoiling arms.
2. Quickly move to fielding position, in line with the ball, as soon as the ball is hit or thrown.
3. On quick release throws, snap the wrist, shift weight forward (time permitting), and follow through.
4. For throwing on the run, position body in line with intended throw, then field and throw without breaking stride.

Common Errors

1. Overrunning the ball when charging grounders.
2. Failure to watch the ball into the glove when preparing for a quick throw.

Teaching Tips and Strategy

1. For fielding and throwing on the run, good timing and a strong arm and wrist must be developed.

Drills

Burn out. Two players face each other approximately 30 feet apart. Using one ball, players throw back and forth as quickly and as hard as possible.

Double ball warm-up. Two players, each with a ball, face one another. Using an overhand throw, players simultaneously throw the ball back and forth.

Bullet. Several runners line up on the first baseline approximately five feet from home plate (Fig. 6.1). The infielders assume their normal positions. The coach hits a firm grounder to any fielder. The fielder charges the ball, fields it, and throws to first base in one motion. The runner attempts to beat the throw to first base.

The Sidearm Throw

Infielders must be able to field balls with a quick release on the throw. The side arm throw enables the quickest release and should be executed for moderate distances, without sacrificing accuracy.

Performance Description

1. Turn the torso so the non-throwing side faces the target.
2. Extend the upper arm diagonally out and down from the shoulder while extending the forearm directly up from the elbow (Fig. 6.2).

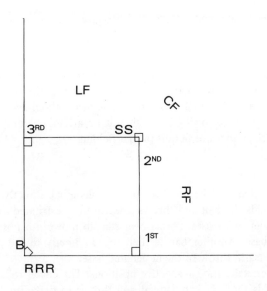

Figure 6.1
Bullet

Figure 6.2
Backswing of a sidearm throw

Figure 6.3
Release on sidearm throw

3. Drop the forearm to a position parallel with the ground as the arm moves forward.
4. Transfer weight to the forward foot and rotate the torso toward the target (Fig. 6.3).
5. As arm moves forward, release the ball with a wrist snap and follow through across the body.

Common Errors

1. Tenseness in the throw.
2. Failure to transfer the weight and snap the wrist to give force to the throw.

Teaching Tips and Strategy

1. Players must have full control of the ball prior to executing the throw.
2. If time does not permit throwing from an upright position, the throw may be made with the trunk bent and the arm moving in a horizontal plane below shoulder level.
3. Fielding the ball with the throwing hand should be attempted only if the ball is stopped or moving slowly, and time does not permit proper fielding.

Drills

Infield throwing and catching. The coach or player rolls a ball directly to an infielder in normal position. The infielder fields the ball and throws sidearm to a designated base. The ball is then rolled to the side of the infielder, who uses a cross-over step to move into position to field the ball and throws to a designated base. Another ball is then rolled directly to the infielder, who from a low position makes a quick sidearm throw to the designated base.

Barehand. The infielders take their respective positions. The coach rolls the ball to each infielder in turn. Each player fields the ball barehanded and throws to first. Emphasis should be placed on fielding and throwing in the same motion.

DEFENSIVE SKILLS: FAST-PITCH PITCHING

Advanced pitching in fast-pitch softball involves controlling the speed, spin, and placement of the ball. The development of an accurate, straight, fastball is basic to a softball pitcher. Once this pitch is mastered, curved balls and various windups add versatility and keep batters uncertain regarding expected pitches.

Fastball

Performance Description

1. Use a tripod grip or the five-fingered grip, if the hand is small.
2. With the ball in front of the body, take a position with both feet in contact with the pitcher's plate.
3. As the backswing is taken, keep the pivot foot in contact with the pitcher's plate, and rotate the trunk slightly away from home plate.
4. Swing the arm back in a pendular motion and forward, extending the elbow and facing the batter on the downswing. Step forward with the opposite foot as the downswing begins (Fig. 6.4).
5. As the ball begins to roll off the fingers below hip level, snap the wrist upward.
6. Follow through with the elbow straight (Fig. 6.5).
7. Assume ready fielding position off the plate.

Common Errors

1. Holding the ball in the palm.
2. Releasing the ball late, resulting in a high pitch.
3. Releasing the ball early resulting in a low pitch.
4. Following through in an off-balanced position.
5. Failure to swing the arm parallel to the body and straight through on the release.

Figure 6.4
Backswing

Figure 6.5
Follow-through

a

b

c

Figure 6.6
Curveball release

Figure 6.7
Windmill

Curveball

Performance Description

1. Grip the ball with the fingers on the outside of the ball (Fig. 6.6).
2. Use footwork as in fastball.
3. On releasing the ball, rotate the arm and hand inward causing the ball to curve right to left, or left to right for left-handed pitchers.
4. Follow through straight ahead with palm facing downward.
5. For an incurve pitch, the arm is rotated outward instead of inward.

Windups

Performance Description

1. **Windmill.** Make a full circle by swinging the arm forward, upward, around, and through by the hip (Fig. 6.7a). Twist the body slightly away from the batter and initiate forward step as the ball is raised (Fig. 6.7b). Do not lock the elbow until the forward swing begins. Whip arm down and through as the body quickly twists towards the batter (Fig. 6.7c). Release the ball with a wrist snap and follow through.
2. **Half windmill.** Bring the ball back, with a bent arm, approximately head high and rotate the body away from home plate (Fig. 6.8a). On the forward step, swing the arm downward and through, turning the body back toward home (Fig. 6.8b). Snap the wrist on the release.

a   b

Figure 6.8
Half windmill

3. **Figure eight.** A figure eight is made by the looping transition from the backswing to the forward swing and the follow-through of the arm. Rotate the trunk toward the throwing side while swinging the pitching hand from a chest-high position, outward, downward, and backward. Continue the motion to a position behind the body. Rotate the trunk to face the batter as the forward swing begins.

Teaching Tips and Strategy

1. Control must come before speed in learning the fast ball.
2. Develop a smooth and efficient style.
3. Modifications in the basic grip and release of the ball account for differences in the flight, speed, and spin of the pitch.
4. At the completion of the follow-through, the pitcher should prepare to field the ball, or assume backing up and covering responsibilities.
5. Be aware of the ability and position of each baserunner.
6. When anticipating a steal, pitch out for a pickoff attempt.
7. When anticipating a bunt, come off the mound and quickly advance toward the batter.

Drills

Fast pitch drill. A target indicating the strike zone is marked on a wall. The pitcher practices pitching to different areas on the target.

Pitcher-vs-pitcher. Two pitchers work as a battery. One player pitches balls to the other who acts as the catcher. The "catcher" calls balls and strikes, with imaginary batters registering strike outs or walks. Any "batter" who receives a walk becomes a "baserunner," and progresses with subsequent walks. After three outs, the pitcher and catcher switch positions to finish the inning. Players compete for the fewest runs in a set number of innings.

DEFENSIVE SKILLS: INFIELD

Advanced players must develop their existing skills in lateral fielding, charging ground balls, throwing on the run, backing up, relaying and covering. In addition, infielders must be familiar with their responsibilities in executing rundowns, cutoffs, and fielding bunted balls in order to maximize defensive team play and avoid confusion when these situations arise.

Rundown

The rundown is used when a baserunner is trapped between two bases. Team effort is necessary as the defensive players close in on the runner from both sides.

Performance Description (Rundown between first and second)

1. The first and second basemen assume positions close to their respective bases. The ball is thrown to the second baseman.
2. The catcher and shortstop back up the basemen.
3. The second baseman forces the runner back toward first base by holding the ball in a throwing position and charging the runner (Fig. 6.9).

Figure 6.9
Rundown

4. The shortstop assumes a position on second base.
5. The second baseman throws to first baseman to tag the runner and retreats to back up the shortstop if the tag is unsuccessful.
6. If the runner changes direction and moves toward second base, the first baseman charges the runner and throws to the shortstop for the tag.
7. If the tag is not successful, the catcher assumes a position on first. The first baseman retreats to back up catcher.

Common Errors

1. Allowing too many throws before attempting the tag.
2. Failure to have runners on other bases under control while attempting the rundown.
3. Not forcing the runner back by charging the runner.
4. Hitting the runner with the ball when throwing.

Teaching Tips and Strategy

1. Proper positioning, backing up, charging the runner and throwing accurately must be emphasized.
2. To eliminate the chance of a throwing error, fielders should attempt to tag the runner in two or less throws. The fielder who is to make the tag should move toward the runner and call for the ball when within tagging range.
3. Fielders should force the runner to retreat toward the base previously passed and make the tag on the runner's back.
4. Fielders participating in a rundown should position themselves slightly to the side of the base path to allow a throwing lane.
5. Before throwing the ball, fielders should force the runner to commit to a particular direction.
6. Care must be taken to prevent other runners from advancing. When attempting a rundown on a player off of first base, a runner on third should not be allowed to score. The second baseman charges the runner near first and either tags or tosses the ball to the first baseman for the putout. The tag is made and the fielder immediately checks the runner or throws to home plate for the tag. If the runner on third is quick and has a good lead off the base, the best option may be to prevent both runners from advancing rather than trying for an out. In this case, the second baseman forces the runner back to first while watching the other runner on third.

Drills

Rundown. A runner is stationed halfway between first and second base. Basemen are positioned on each bag. The ball starts at first base and is thrown to second. Players will attempt a rundown. This drill also may be practiced between second and third, and third and home. Outfielders and pitchers not acting as fielders in the rundown may serve as trapped runners.

Fielding the Bunt

Infielders must be able to anticipate bunting situations, and have a plan of action for fielding the ball or covering a base without hesitation.

Figure 6.10
Fielding a bunt

Performance Description

1. Anticipating the bunt, the first and third basemen charge toward the batter as the ball is pitched.
2. As the ball reaches the plate, assume a ready position.
3. The ball is quickly scooped up (Fig. 6.10), or barehanded, and a sidearm throw is made.
4. Second baseman and shortstop cover appropriate bases for putout attempts.

Common Errors

1. Confusion in determining which player should field the bunt.
2. Failure to properly field a spinning ball.
3. Hesitating too long before deciding where to make the play.

Teaching Tips and Strategy

1. With the first and third basemen charging in, the second baseman covers first base and the shortstop covers second base. The left fielder may then cover third base for any play at that bag.
2. Know the bunting ability and speed of opponents and learn to anticipate bunting situations.
3. The fielder of the bunt should throw to the appropriate base, rather than throwing to the fielder who is moving to cover the base.
4. Attempts should be made to put out the lead runner. If a lead runner putout is doubtful, the fielder should play for the sure out.

Drills

Bunt coverage. First and third basemen assume close-in positions. When the ball is pitched, a batter attempts to hit a bunt either down the first baseline, the third baseline or in front of the plate. Each batter attempts five bunts. On each bunt the fielders practice charging the ball or assuming their base covering positions. Baserunners may be added to this drill to simulate game situations.

Cutoff

Generally, players need much practice and experience to effectively decide whether or not a cutoff should be made. The purpose of the cutoff is to intercept and redirect a throw to put out a baserunner at a base other than the throw's original designation. Frequently, a player will cut off a throw to a base when it appears the throw will be unsuccessful in putting out a runner. By cutting off the ball, the fielder may prevent another runner from advancing, or may trap the advancing runner off base.

Performance Description

1. A designated infielder calls for all cutoffs on throws from outfielders.
2. The cutoff player assumes a position approximately 20-25 feet in front of the intended target.
3. The cutoff player judges the possible success of the throw. If unsuccessful, the fielder intervenes and redirects the ball for another possibility.

Common Errors

1. Cutting off a throw which could have resulted in a putout.
2. Failure to designate an infielder to call for cutoffs.

Teaching Tips and Strategy

1. Cutoffs on throws from right field to home are usually taken by the first baseman or pitcher. The player (pitcher or first baseman) not executing the cutoff backs up home plate. Throws from left field to home are cut off by the pitcher or shortstop. The catcher, having a good view of the situation calls for the cutoff and redirection.
2. A catcher's throw to second base on stealing attempts may be cut off by the pitcher, second baseman, or shortstop when a runner is on third base. A good cutoff player throws immediately back to the catcher. Consequently, the runner at third may be trapped off the base for a putout, or the runner may be forced back to the base.

Drill

Cutoff. Defensive players take their respective positions in the field. The coach sets the situation by placing the runners on bases. As the batter hits a pitched ball, runners try to advance on base hits to the outfield. The catcher calls the plays: "Cut first," "cut second," or "cut third." "Cut" directs the cutoff player to catch the ball, and "first," "second," or "third" suggests the new direction for the throw. If a call is not made, the throw comes home uninterrupted.

Improving Infield Skills

The following complex drills offer new applications for practicing strategic concepts and techniques previously introduced.

Drills

Wide throws to first. The coach or thrower takes a position two-thirds of the way to the shortstop position. Throws are alternated to the right and to the left of first base, forcing the baseman to stretch to make the catch.

Covering your bag. A ground ball is fungo hit to each infielder. The fielder throws the ball to first. The first baseman throws to the catcher. The catcher then throws to the base for which the infielder is responsible. The shortstop will cover second base upon return from the catcher. The ball is then thrown around the horn to the catcher. The process is repeated for each infielder.

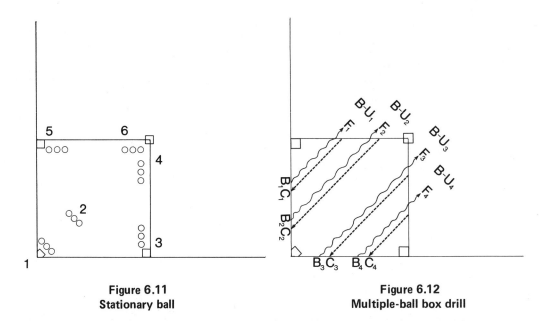

Figure 6.11
Stationary ball

Figure 6.12
Multiple-ball box drill

Force play. The coach dictates a situation and the infielders take appropriate positions: normal, shallow, or deep. One runner is placed on first base. Additional runners are lined up outside the foul line at first base. The coach hits a ball to a fielder. The fielder executes a force play at second. Runners may be placed on first and second; or first, second, and third to increase the difficulty of the drill.

Stationary ball. Infielders are placed as indicated in the diagram (Fig. 6.11). Several softballs are placed six feet apart and ten feet in front of the infielder. The coach calls three numbers corresponding to positions in the infield. Example: The coach calls five, four, and three. The first number is the position of the player, and the second and third numbers indicate where the ball should be thrown. In this situation, the third baseman picks up one ball and throws to the second baseman who is covering second base. The second baseman then throws to the first baseman for a double play.

Multiple-ball box drill. The formation is basically the same as the *one-ball box drill* except the batter hits to a different fielder (Fig. 6.12). The batter closest to third hits grounders to the fielder in shallow left field. The batter on the first base side of home plate hits grounders to the second baseman. The batter nearest first base hits to the fielder in shallow right field. The batter hits the second ball as the fielder throws the first ball to the catcher. The batter also place-hits the grounders to allow the fielder practice in lateral coverage.

The loop. Infielders line up at the third base coach's box (Fig. 6.13). Fielders are positioned at first, second, and home. Several balls are placed on the ground two feet from the pitcher's plate on the third base side. An infielder takes a position at third base. The batter fungo hits a ground ball to the third baseman. The player fields the ball, throws to first base, runs to the mound, picks up the placed ball and throws to second. After the throw, the player runs the shortstop position, fields a looping fly ball (which has been hit or thrown by the coach), and throws it to the catcher.

Continuous fielding. The batter fungo hits consecutive balls to the third baseman. Immediately following the throw to home another ball is hit to the fielder. The player continues to field the ball and throw to home until four fielding or throwing errors, or 20 successful plays have been made. Continue the drill with each position. Players should not try to pick up mishandled balls.

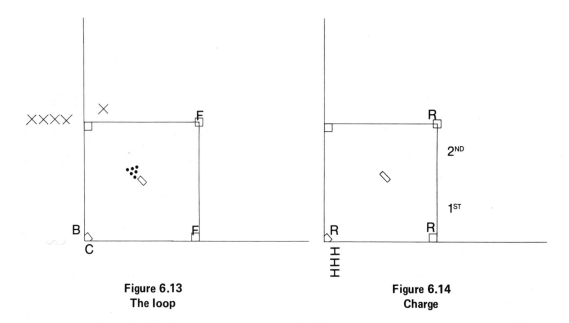

Figure 6.13
The loop

Figure 6.14
Charge

Suicide. The infielder assumes a normal fielding position. The batter hits 15 grounders in a row or as many as it takes for the fielder to make five consecutive plays without an error. Each play consists of a clean pick up and accurate throw to a designated base.

Triple. The coach assigns players to infield positions with remaining players lining up as baserunners behind home plate. When the ball is hit, the runner sprints to first, rounds second, and runs to third. As the runner is running, the coach hits two balls in rapid succession to the same infielder. The hits are timed so the second hit is executed when the first throw is made to first base, the third hit is made when the second throw is made to second. As the runner rounds the bases, the first throw goes to first, the second throw goes to second, and the third throw goes to third base. The perfect play is an out at each base.

Running fungo. Players with their gloves on are stationed at second and third base. Other players, also with gloves on, line up at home. The first player runs at full speed to first base. As the runner rounds the base going to second, the coach hits a grounder between first and second. The runner fields the ball, throws to second and continues around second toward third. A second ball is hit between second and third. The runner fields the ball and throws it to third. The runner assumes the third baseman's position. The third baseman rotates to second base and the second baseman rotates to the end of the baserunner's line.

Charge. Runners are placed at home, first base, and second base, with remaining runners lined up behind home facing first base (Fig. 6.14). Fielders assume the first baseman and second baseman positions. Infielders line up one behind the other on first base side of home plate facing third base. When the coach calls "go," the first infielder on the first base line races for third. When the infielder is midway between home and third, the runner on second breaks for third. Once at third base, the infielder turns to face the catcher who throws the ball to third. As the catch is made at third, the runner at first breaks for second base. The fielder makes the tag at third, throws to second, then runs across the diamond toward first base. The fielder at second makes the tag and *holds* the ball. As the infielder passes the pitcher's plate, the runner at home runs for first base. The coach hits a grounder just inside the first baseline. The infielder moving toward first base fields the ball, throws to first base for the out and goes to the end of the baserunners' line. Baserunners from second go to the end of the infielders' line. Upon completion of the play the runners at first and second remain on their base. A new runner takes a position at home.

Double triangle. The double triangle drill has four phases of infield practice (Fig. 6.15). Batter, catcher, and infielders assume the described positions.

Phase 1. All infielders except the pitcher assume their respective positions. A batter and catcher assume positions, behind the baseline, halfway between home and first base. Another batter and catcher assume a comparable position on the third base line between home and third. The batter on the first base line fungo hits grounders to the shortstop who throws to first base. The ball is then returned to the appropriate catcher. The batter on the third base line fungo hits a ground ball to the second baseman who throws to the third baseman. The ball is then returned to the appropriate catcher.

Phase 2. The batter on the third base line hits a slow grounder to the first baseman who fields the ball and throws to the shortstop covering second. The shortstop then returns the ball to the appropriate catcher. The batter on the first base line hits a slow grounder to the third baseman who fields the ball and then throws to the second baseman covering first base. The ball is then returned to the appropriate catcher.

Phase 3. The batter on the first base side hits to the shortstop who tosses the ball to the second baseman covering the bag. The second baseman returns the ball to the catcher. The batter on the third base line hits to the first baseman who throws to the third baseman on the base. The third baseman returns the ball to the catcher.

Phase 4. The batter on the first base line hits a grounder to the third baseman who throws to first. The first baseman returns the ball to catcher. The batter on the third base line hits a ground ball to the second baseman who tosses the ball to the shortstop covering second. The shortstop returns the ball to catcher.

DEFENSIVE SKILLS: OUTFIELD

Outfielders must be conditioned to execute correctly previously taught outfield skills, including positioning for the catch, backing up infielders, throwing to a relay player, and fielding deep hits. Instinctively, players should back up adjacent outfielders and charge forward on balls hit to infielders in front of them. Frequently they must serve as relay players to assist other fielders. Cooperation must exist between adjacent outfielders and between infielders and outfielders to prevent collisions and mishandling of the ball in overlap areas. In addition to judging the velocity and direction of a batted ball, outfielders must know their own speed and capabilities in determining whether a shoestring catch, or allowing the ball to bounce before the catch is more appropriate. Misjudging hard-hit balls can result in an error which allows the runner more bases than deserved.

Performance Description

1. When not involved in catching or backing up, move into a position for a possible relay on deep hits.
2. If it appears the baserunner will not advance beyond the base approached, and a play cannot be made on the runner, immediately bring the ball to throwing position and run toward the base to which the runner is advancing.

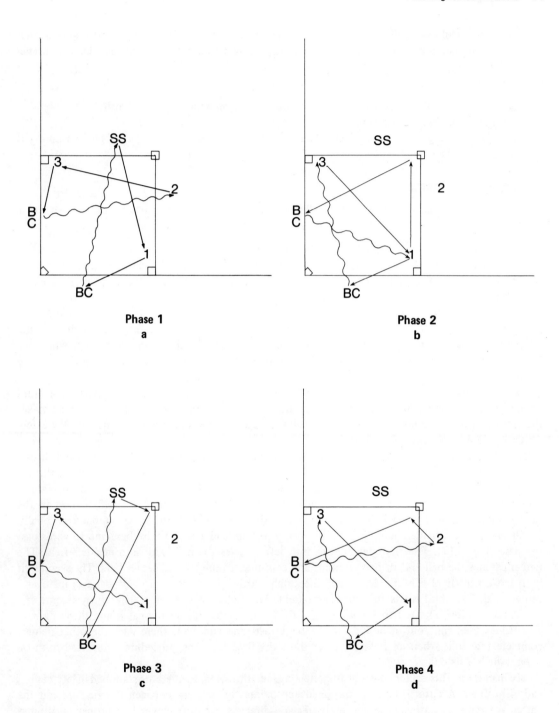

Figure 6.15
Double triangle

3. Throw the ball low to the base ahead of a runner when a tag is to be attempted. If it appears that the baserunner will advance beyond the base approached, throw to the next base closest to home.

Common Errors

1. Not calling for balls hit between fielders or not heeding an adjacent fielder's call.
2. Throwing "behind the baserunner."
3. Failure to use good judgment regarding the choice between throwing the ball or running it into the infield.

Teaching Tips and Strategy

1. Appropriate signals should be taught to all fielders to eliminate confusion on balls hit between them.

Drills

Shoestring catches. Outfielders line up in center field. The coach and catcher stand on the left field foul line. On signal, the fielder runs directly toward the coach. The coach throws a low, sinking line drive directly at the fielder. The fielder catches, blocks, or traps the ball and throws it to the catcher.

Charge, scoop, throw. Outfielders line up in single file at one outfield position or take their respective positions in the outfield (Fig. 6.16). The ball is batted to the fielder from the pitcher's plate. Charging the ball at top speed, the outfielder assumes a position in line with the target to which the ball is to be thrown. The ball is caught and an overhand throw is made without losing the forward momentum. Baserunners may be used to make the drill more realistic.

Tag-up throw. Runners line up in the third base coaching box. One runner takes a position at third base. Fielders assume normal positions. A coach fungo hits a fly into short left field. The fielder makes the catch and throws the ball home in an attempt to put out the runner who advances on the catch. This procedure is continued for all fielders.

Non-stop. Batter hits 20 consecutive balls to the outfielder. The player fields the ball and throws in the following pattern: first ball is thrown home; second ball is thrown to third; third ball is thrown to second; and fourth ball is thrown to first. Basemen return all balls to catcher. Each hit is made simultaneously with the throw from the previous catch. A prompter may be used to remind the fielder where to throw the ball. The catcher counts the hits and keeps the batter supplied with balls.

All the way. Outfielders line up in foul territory perpendicular to the third base line 15 yards past the base (Fig. 6.17). The first fielder runs into left field as the ball is hit into mid-left field. The fielder catches the ball and throws to home and continues to run toward center field. The second hit is to left-center field. The fielder makes the catch, throws to home, and continues to run toward center field. The third hit is to right-center field. The fielder makes the catch, throws home and continues running. The fourth hit is to right field. The fielder makes the catch and throws home. The fielder then runs out-of-bounds at the right field line and waits there until the other fielders complete the drill. When all fielders are at the right field line, the procedure is reversed to move toward the left field line.

Six-man slam. This drill involves hitting, fielding, and throwing. Fielders are stationed in left, center, and right field. A cutoff player is stationed approximately midway between the fielders and the batter. A catcher is stationed beside the batter and directs the cutoff player to a proper position as the batter hits to left field. The batter then fungo hits the next ball to center field and so on. Players rotate one position after each batter has hit balls to every fielder twice.

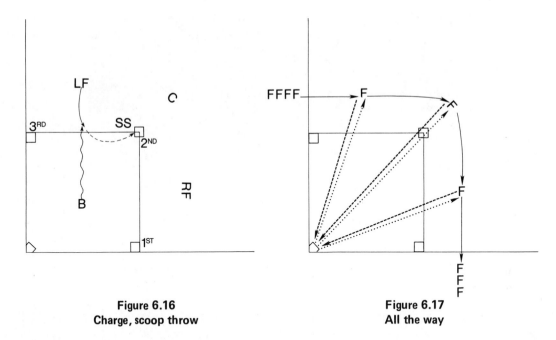

Figure 6.16
Charge, scoop throw

Figure 6.17
All the way

OFFENSIVE SKILLS: BATTING

Bunting

In fast-pitch softball, having players who can bunt the ball gives a team a vital offensive weapon. A bunt is a surprise tactic frequently used when infielders are playing deep in their positions. More often bunting is employed to draw the first baseman and third baseman in, close to the plate, when a runner is on base, usually first. With the baserunner advancing on the pitch, the fielder has insufficient time to make a successful play on the runner and must throw to first base for the putout. Moreover, with the first and third basemen and pitcher charging in, confusion in fielding the bunt, or covering the bases, may result in a defensive error. Thus, the properly executed sacrifice bunt safely places a baserunner in scoring position. Likewise, the squeeze bunt, which requires a highly competent batter, may be used to advance a fast runner from third to home. The deceptive fake bunt is most appropriately employed when a runner is stealing third base. This manuever draws the third baseman in and away from the base and may distract the catcher, thus delaying the quick throw to the bag. A slap hit may be used to pull the defense in close to assist a baserunner in stealing or to allow the batter to hit the ball just over the charging infielder's head.

Performance Description

1. Grip bat firmly with the bottom hand.
2. Support bat loosely with the top hand sliding to a position midway up the bat. Place the thumb on top, with the fingers supporting under, and parallel to, the bat (away from the hitting surface).
3. As the ball is released, pivot, with feet slightly apart, to face the pitcher.
4. Square the shoulders and position the bat parallel, or at a slight angle, to the ground (Fig. 6.18).

Figure 6.18
Bunting

Figure 6.19
Drag bunt

5. Angle bat with top hand on contact to direct the ball to the right, left, or center.
6. "Give" with the arms and bat while contacting the ball in front of the plate.
7. To execute a drag bunt, assume a normal batting stance, without stride, and tap the ball down the appropriate baseline (Fig. 6.19). Right-handed batters should direct the ball down the third base line, and left-handed batters should place it down the first base line.
8. To execute a slap hit, during the wind-up assume a bunting position, then quickly assume a normal batting position. Bring the bat back quickly and swing at the ball.
9. To fake bunt, assume a bunting position deep in the batter's box, but do not contact the ball.

Common Errors

1. Placing the top hand's fingers around the bat, vulnerable to the oncoming ball.
2. Failure to "give with the ball" on contact.
3. Popping the ball up in the air due to failure to contact the ball squarely with the bat.
4. Failure to disguise the bunt prior to release of the pitch.
5. On a sacrifice or squeeze bunt, failure to contact the ball.

Teaching Tips and Strategy

1. Low pitches are easiest to bunt.
2. To promote "giving" upon contact, players should "catch the ball with the bat."
3. Players should practice directing the ball down opposite foul lines.
4. Generally, bunters should go with the pitch. Inside pitches should be bunted toward first base and outside pitches toward third.
5. A fake hit may be followed with a slap hit. Once infielders are drawn in, a slap hit will direct the ball just over their heads. The slap hit is made with a short, quick backswing.
6. To advance a runner to second, a bunt is hit in the direction of the fielder who would have the most difficult throw to second.
7. The sacrifice bunt should be used when there are no outs, the game is close or runners are on first, first and second, or second base.

Drills

Bunting drill. Four players participate in this drill: a pitcher, two fielders, and a batter. One fielder is positioned on the first base line and the other fielder on the third base line. The batter bunts eight or ten pitched balls, after which players rotate one position clockwise.

Reaction bunting. At close range a pitcher throws overhand to a batter, who attempts to bunt the ball in designated directions. Ten attempts are allowed each batter.

Squeeze bunt drill. Infielders assume a "close in" position with a runner on third base. A pitched ball is bunted to the ground and the runner attempts to advance. If the ball is popped up the runner returns to third. Pitcher, catcher, first and third basemen all move to play the bunted ball. The direction of the bunt will be varied in successive attempts.

Place Hitting

Once the basic batting technique is mastered a batter must strive to place hit the ball into open areas of the field, down the foul lines, or between fielders. By adjusting the point of contact, the stance, or the follow-through, the batter may be able to direct the ball toward less skilled players, or hit behind a runner to permit further advancement.

Performance Description

1. From normal batting position, move the forward foot to an open or closed stance (Figs. 6.20, 6.21).
2. Hit to the opposite field by closing the stance, swinging "late," and letting the follow-through angle the bat toward the desired field.
3. To pull a ball, open the stance, contact the ball in front of the body, break the wrists sharply, and forcefully follow through (Fig. 6.22).

Figure 6.20
Closed stance

Figure 6.21
Open stance

Figure 6.22
Hitting to opposite field

4. To hit the ball straight away, or to center field, assume a normal stance and make contact with the ball when it is even with the forward hip.
5. For hitting a greater distance, use a long grip, swing forcefully and follow through slightly upward.

Common Errors

1. Failure to consider location of the pitch in determining the place hitting direction (failure to "go with the pitch").
2. Improper execution in "hitting behind" a runner to the opposite field.
3. Attempting to hit a long ball instead of place-hitting safely.
4. Stepping across the plate or out of the batter's box before making contact.

Teaching Tips and Strategy

1. "Choking up" on fast balls permits a quicker, more controlled swing.
2. Right-handed batters should pull inside pitches to left field and hit outside pitches to right field.
3. "Hitting behind the runner" places the ball away from the direction of the advancing runner.

Drills

Place hitting. Mark off a zone of 15 feet on each side of second base. Six players (three fielders, one pitcher, one catcher, and one batter) are involved in the drill (Fig. 6.23). Each batter has six swings. The object is to score the most points. One point is scored for each hit into the target zone. The players should rotate after the batter completes six swings. Zones may be established in any field.

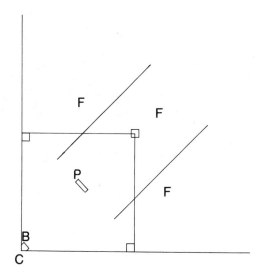

Figure 6.23
Place hitting

a   b

Figure 6.24
Fungo hitting

Fungo Hitting

One technique that utilizes the fundamentals of place hitting is fungo hitting. Fungo hitting may develop batting strength and improve eye-hand coordination. Although not used in actual play, the skill is appropriate for hitting balls to infielders or outfielders in practice or warm-up situations.

Performance Description

1. Hold the ball in the non-dominant hand, waist high, in front of the body.
2. With the dominant hand, grasp the bat approximately six to ten inches up the grip and hold the bat back and away from the shoulder.
3. Toss the ball upward and approximately four feet from the body (Fig. 6.24a).
4. Immediately place the non-dominant hand below the other hand on the grip.
5. Keep the eye on the ball, and time the full swing to meet the ball as it drops (Fig. 6.24b).
6. Follow through.

Common Errors

1. Not placing the non-dominant hand on the bat.
2. Not tossing the ball far enough away from the body or at a sufficient height to allow for a full swing.

Drills

1. Practice hitting balls to designated infielders or outfielders.
2. Using the fungo technique, apply the place hitting drill.

Improving Batting Skills

The following drills add game-like elements to practicing batting skills.

Drills

Rotational batting. Three teams of five players each are formed. Team A is at bat. Team B positions a battery, first baseman, second baseman, and right fielder to the right side of the field. Team C positions the third baseman, shortstop, left fielder, center fielder, and short fielder to the left side of the field. Team A attempts to score against teams B and C. Team A bats until three outs are made. Team B then bats as Team A rotates to the left side of the field, and Team C rotates to the right side of the field and furnishes the battery. Play continues until each team has had a turn at bat.

Four-player team. An offensive team consisting of four players attempts to score against a full defensive team. Players continue their turn at bat until three outs are made.

DEFENSIVE SKILLS: BASERUNNING

A thorough knowledge of running bases will undoubtedly earn extra runs for a team. Batters and baserunners should be aware of each situation and follow appropriate baserunning patterns. Advanced instruction should include the proper use of the lead-off, hit and run, steal and slide.

Lead-off

In fast pitch softball, the baserunner should lead off the base as soon as the ball leaves the pitcher's hand. The lead-off should be the greatest distance that allows the baserunner to return to the base safely in case of a pickoff attempt. Slow pitch rules do not allow the player to leave the base until the ball crosses home plate or is hit.

Performance Description

1. Assume a take-off position facing the next base with body low and weight forward.
2. Place the left foot in a push-off position on the inside corner of the base.
3. Without hesitation, take several steps off the base at the moment permitted by the rules (Fig. 6.25).
4. As the lead-off is taken, focus the eyes on home plate to determine if the ball is hit or misplayed by the catcher.
5. If the ball is thrown back to the pitcher and no opportunity for stealing is present, quickly return to the base and repeat the process on the next pitch.
6. Alternate method:
   a. Place the left foot on the base with the right foot behind the base (Fig. 6.26).
   b. Step forward with the rear foot prior to the pitcher's release (fast pitch).

Figure 6.25
Lead-off

Figure 6.26
Alternate lead-off position

Common Errors

1. Leading off the base too soon.
2. Failure to return to the base quickly when a steal is not attempted, resulting in being trapped between bases.
3. Underestimating or overestimating personal capabilities and speed in taking a lead-off.

Teaching Tips and Strategy

1. After leading off, advance without hesitation when a ground ball is hit.
2. On a line drive, the runner should delay the advance to see if the ball is caught. If the ball is not caught, the runner should proceed rapidly. If caught, a quick return to the base must be made. Players must be alert to opportunities to tag up and run.
3. Runners must know the greatest distance a lead-off may be taken safely. Due to the throwing distance from home to second base, a longer lead-off may be taken from second than from other bases.
4. If a long fly ball is hit, the runner should take a lengthy lead-off and observe if the ball is caught or in play; then advance or return to the base. If the runner is on second or third bases, a coach may assist by signalling to return or advance.
5. With less than two outs, on a shallow-hit ball to a fielder with a strong throwing arm, faking a sprint home can draw the throw.
6. Lead-offs from third base should be taken in foul territory to avoid the runner being struck by a fair ball.

Drills

Lead-off. Players assume fielding positions. Runner on first base practices leading off when the ball is pitched. If the ball is a base hit, the runner quickly reacts by running to the next base. If the ball is caught, the runner returns to the base.

Hit-and-Run

The hit-and-run is a predetermined play in which the baserunner advances with the expectation that the batter will hit the ball. The batter's intent is to hit the ball into an area vacated by a fielder moving to cover the base to which the baserunner is advancing. Frequently, the play is used with a runner on first to advance the runner a minimum of two bases. The fast takeoff gives the runner an advantage in reaching the bases safely and limits the double play possibility. The hit-and-run is effective in scoring a runner from third when the fielders are moving in anticipation of a squeeze bunt. A prerequisite for the hit-and-run is a fast runner and a dependable batter who can hit hard ground balls.

Performance Description

1. The hit-and-run signal is given by the third-base coach.
2. On the pitch, the baserunner charges to the next base.
3. As the baseman moves to cover the base of the advancing runner, the batter hits to the baseman's original position.

Common Errors

1. Batter does not attempt to hit the pitch.
2. Batter hits a sharp line drive which is caught by a fielder who then puts out the baserunner for a double play.
3. Ball is popped up on an infield fly.
4. Baserunner hesitates after leaving the base.

Teaching Tips

1. Preferably the batter should hit a ground ball.

Drill

Baserunner's suicide. The entire team lines up single file at home plate. Using a staggered start, all players sprint to first base as if a single had been hit. After all players reach first base, players individually assume a baserunner's position. Players then advance on the coach's command and stop on third base. As baserunners on third, players sprint home. From the home plate position, runners advance to second base as if a double were hit, then sprint directly home. The drill continues as runners go for a triple, and finally for a home run. It is important that all baserunners maintain a staggered start throughout the drill. Using runners only on first or third, this drill may be used to practice the hit-and-run.

Figure 6.27
Stealing

Figure 6.28
Baserunner preparing to slide into second base

Stealing (Fast-Pitch Only)

Base stealing is a technique which advances runners into better scoring positions through speed, alertness, and cunning. Instruction in the appropriate opportunities and techniques of stealing will enhance success. A baserunner who is a stealing threat is often distracting to a pitcher and catcher and may cause a loss of concentration on the pitch. Consequently, the threat alone can force errors by the defensive team. Good baserunners analyze the pitcher, catcher, and infielders for weaknesses in protecting against the steal, and take advantage of any vulnerabilities.

Performance Description

1. From a lead-off position on base, sprint toward the next base without hesitation as the ball is pitched (Fig. 6.27).
2. If the play is made to the base approached, slide.

Common Errors

1. Not breaking quickly from the base.
2. Watching the ball instead of focusing the eyes ahead.
3. Hesitating after initially leaving the base.

Teaching Tips and Strategy

1. A delayed steal may be attempted by swift runners:
   a. After the lead-off on a pitch, if the catcher does not force the runner back to the base, the runner should advance as the ball is thrown back to the pitcher.
   b. With runners on first and third bases, and less than two outs, the runner on first base takes a long lead-off to draw a throw. The runner advances if the throw is made to first or no throw is attempted. If the throw is made to second, the runner retreats to first, or stops momentarily attempting to draw the fielder's attention and allowing the runner on third to score.

2. Double stealing may be effective and distracting to the opponents. With runners on first and third and less than two outs, both runners break and advance simultaneously.
3. Good strategy includes stealing if the catcher has a weak throwing arm or a slow delivery, and if infielders do not cover their bases properly.
4. Avoid overrunning other baserunners.

Drills

Double-steal drill. Runners are positioned on first and third bases. As the pitcher delivers to the catcher, the runners attempt to advance. The catcher then makes a play on either runner.

Continuous stealing. With players in the field, a runner is placed on first base. As the pitcher releases the ball to a batter, the runner is instructed to steal on a particular pitch or allowed to make an individual decision. Whether safe or out, the runner assumes a position on second and attempts to steal third. Once at third, the runner attempts to steal home. The batter does not attempt to hit any pitches.

Sliding

An advanced player should slide on close plays at any base except when advancing to first. The slide reduces the target for a fielder's tag, and prevents the baserunner from overrunning second or third base without losing speed in the approach (Fig. 6.28). Three commonly used slides will be described. The straight-leg slide has the basic low, straight in approach to the bag. If in doubt about the closeness of the play, the bent-leg slide is recommended. Upon completion of this slide, the runner is standing and ready to advance to the next base. In order to avoid a tag, the hook slide is made to one side of the base.

Performance Description

1. Straight-leg slide
   a. Initiate the slide approximately ten feet from the base.
   b. Lean back, and extend either leg forward and upward.
   c. Bend the other leg at the knee under the extended leg (Fig. 6.29).
   d. Slide along the ground on the bottom leg and hip.
   e. Keep the forward leg and arms off the ground.
2. Bent-leg slide
   a. Initiate the slide about five feet from the base.
   b. Check the backward fall.
   c. Bend the nonsliding, forward leg at the knee.
   d. Bend the sliding leg under the other leg (Fig. 6.30).
   e. As soon as the forward leg touches the bag, thrust the arms and body weight forward, and push the body upward with the sliding leg to a standing position.
3. Hook slide
   a. Initiate the slide with either foot, as in the straight-leg slide.
   b. Lean backward.
   c. Turn the body to the side away from the tag.
   d. Bend the knee of the leg nearest the base and hook the base with the toes (Fig. 6.31).

Figure 6.29
Straight-leg slide

Figure 6.30
Bent-leg slide

Figure 6.31
Hook slide

Common Errors

1. Catching the cleats in the ground while sliding.
2. Falling back on the hands, wrists and fingers resulting in possible injury.
3. Initiating the slide too early or late.

Teaching Tips and Strategy

1. For safety purposes, players should wear long pants or long socks when practicing or playing.
2. Know where to start the slide in relation to the bases.
3. Once the slide is started, continue until completion.
4. Flatten the body while going down to prevent sliding abrasions.
5. Watch the base and not the ball.
6. Keep hands closed on the slide.

Drills

Soft sliding. Using proper technique, players may practice sliding on a grassy area, in a sand pit, or on a tumbling mat.

Repeated slides. Players line up ten feet from a base. Individually, players take the appropriate number of steps and go into a sliding position. The distance and speed of the slide is gradually increased with each attempt.

SAMPLE LESSON PLANS

Day 1 a. Psychomotor assessment

Day 2 a. Review throwing and catching
     b. Introduce sidearm throw
     c. Introduce new infield skills
       and strategies

Day 3 a. Practice outfield skills
       and strategies
     b. Introduce fast-pitch pitching

Day 4 a. Introduce new batting skills:
       bunting, fungo, and place hitting

Day 5 a. Introduce new baserunning skills
       and base coaching
     b. Play softball

Day 6 a. Review previous skills through
       selected drills

Day 7 a. Play softball

Day 8 a. Discuss rules
     b. Practice skills through circuit training

Day 9 a. Introduce scorekeeping
     b. Introduce officiating
     c. Play softball

Day 10 a. Quiz
      b. Review skills through drills

Day 11 a. Pretournament practice

Day 12 a. Tournament

Day 13 a. Tournament

Day 14 a. Tournament

Day 15 a. Tournament

Day 16 a. Tournament

Day 17 a. Tournament

Day 18 a. Psychomotor assessment

Day 19 a. Psychomotor assessment
      b. Cognitive review

Day 20 a. Cognitive evaluation

PROJECTS FOR THE PROSPECTIVE TEACHER/COACH

1. Attend a softball game and record statistics for each team.
2. Observe a teacher instructing an advanced class and evaluate the instructional techniques.
3. Observe the motivational and instructional problems in teaching students with advanced skills and compare with those of instructing a class with beginner skills.
4. Observe a qualified official and analyze the techniques in regard to positioning, making calls, working with the other officials, and controlling the game.

7

Lead-up and Modified Softball Games

LEAD-UP GAMES

When introducing basic skills to young players, the use of lead-up games combines skill practice with the enjoyment of game play. By emphasizing correct form in executing the particular skills required for each game, the instructor is afforded a motivational supplement to drill practice. During the early skill developmental stages, repeated skill applications provide the necessary foundation for later regulation game play.

Twenty one. (Develops throwing, baserunning, and fielding skills) With all fielders in regular fielding positions, the batter throws the ball overhand into fair territory. Following the throw, the batter runs and touches as many bases as possible before a fielder makes a tag with the ball or touches the base to which the runner is advancing. The runner must continue running until being put out or reaching home base. A point is scored for each base the runner successfully passes. With each new batter, the fielders rotate one position. After every member of the team bats, the teams change places. The first team to attain 21 points wins the game.

Throw softball. (Develops catching, throwing, baserunning, and fielding skills) Six to eight players may be assigned to a team. The object of the game is to run the bases without being put out. Instead of batting the ball, the batter catches the pitch and throws it into the field. The game is then played as regulation softball. If the batter drops the ball in the strike zone, throws a foul ball or misses a base, the player is out.

Hit pin softball. (Develops batting, baserunning, fielding, and throwing skills) Two teams may play, each consisting of eight to ten players. Using a diamond with 45-foot baselines, an Indian club is placed at the outside corner of each base and in the middle of home plate. Fielders scatter with a pitcher, catcher, and baseman at each base. After batting the ball into fair territory, the runner attempts to circle the outside of the bases and touch home plate before the fielders can throw the ball to first, second, third, and home consecutively. The baseman at each base must catch the ball and knock over the pin with a foot before throwing to the next base. If all four pins are knocked over before the runner gets home, an out is scored. One point is awarded for each home run.

Around the horn. (Develops baserunning and throwing skills) Eight players per team may participate. Two fielders are stationed at each of the diamond's four bases. The ball starts at home with the catcher. As the runner runs from home to round the bases, the catcher throws to first. The base must be tagged with a foot by the first baseman and then relayed to second. At each base the same procedure must be followed until the ball is returned to the catcher. The fielders must throw the ball around the bases twice before the runner tags all bases and reaches home. One fielder at the base catches the first throw and the second fielder catches the second round throw. One point is scored for each successful run. Teams change sides after all members have a turn, or after a designated number of outs.

One old cat. (Develops batting, baserunning, and fielding skills) Three or more players may participate in this game. The batter attempts to stay at bat as long as possible. The batter must hit the ball and run to first base and back to home plate before the ball is returned to the catcher. If the batter scores five runs (to first base and back scores one run) before being put out, the players rotate: batter to right field, right to center field, center to left field, left to third base, third to shortstop, short to second base, second to first base, first to pitcher, pitcher to catcher, and catcher to batter. Catching a fly ball automatically puts a fielder up to bat. The batter goes to the end of the rotation and other players move up to fill the vacant position of the fielder who caught the ball. The player with the most runs wins the game.

Peggy. (Develops batting and fielding skills) Unlimited fielders scatter in an open playing area. A batter, catcher, and pitcher assume regular positions. The object of the game is to become the batter. This goal may be attained by any *one* of several means:

1. Catching a batted fly ball.
2. Catching a batted ball that has taken only one bounce.
3. Catching five batted ground balls (without fumbling) hit by one batter. Ground balls are not cumulative when a batter change occurs.
4. The catcher catches two balls that have been swung at and missed by the same batter.

Team pepper. (Develops batting, pitching, and fielding skills) With eight to ten players on a team, each team forms a circle with one batter in the center. Each player around the circle takes a turn at pitching a ball to the center batter who place hits the ball to the player on the pitcher's left. If the batter misses the ball, it must be returned to the player who pitched the ball. If the fielder misses the ball, the batter must rehit the ball to that fielder before continuing. A round consists of everyone on the team having an opportunity to bat. The team that finishes the round first is declared the winner.

MODIFIED GAMES

Due to the limited time of class sessions, the increasing coeducational nature of physical education and recreational play, and the skill differences among the players, adaptations in the official game may be desirable. Two popular examples of modified games, suitable for all levels of play, are one-pitch softball and co-recreational softball. A third game, sixteen-inch softball requires greater strength in the execution of throwing and batting skills.

One-pitch softball. To speed up play one-pitch softball is recommended. The pitcher is furnished by the batting team. A member of the fielding team is positioned in the proximity of the pitcher's mound for fielding purposes. The following rules apply:

1. Since the batter and pitcher are teammates, the pitcher will attempt to throw good pitches and the batter is expected to hit the first pitch.
2. The batter is out if the ball is missed, hit foul, or if a swing is not attempted.
3. Stealing and bunting are prohibited.

4. Players are expected to run on and off the field.
5. For any delay by the batting team in getting the batter or pitcher ready, an out is declared.
6. As soon as the pitcher and batter are in place, the ball may be pitched. This encourages the fielders to assume their positions readily.
7. Official softball rules are applied in all other situations.

Co-recreational softball. Co-recreational softball is a popular game in which men and women play on the same team competitively. Rule modifications are made primarily to equalize any skill differences that may be found between men and women players. The number and degree of modifications made depend on factors such as skill, age of the players, and purpose of the game. In situations where the skill level is high, the only changes may be in the determination of the number of men and women on a team and allowing pinch hitters to be used only for the same sex. In situations where the skill level between men and women needs to be equalized, more extreme modifications may be desirable. Examples of modifications that may be appropriate include the following:

1. Pitching a 16-inch softball to men batters and a regulation softball to women batters.
2. Men batters must bat from the non-preferred side of the plate, e.g., men that customarily hit from the right-hand side of the plate must hit from the left-hand side.
3. Male and female batters must be alternated in the batting order.
4. Sliding is not permitted.

Sixteen-inch softball. By replacing the standard 12-inch ball with an official 16-inch ball the batter is given a larger target. Less playing space is needed, and fielders are assisted by a decrease in the flight and speed of the larger ball. Rules are similar to the 12-inch slow-pitch rules with a few exceptions:[1]

1. The baselines are reduced to 55 feet (18.15 meters) for men and 50 feet (16.5 meters) for women, if desired.
2. The pitching plate is 38 feet (12.54 meters) from home plate.
3. The pitcher may use two hesitation pitches prior to the mandatory pitch.
4. The pitcher's foot may be in contact with the pitcher's plate when a pickoff is attempted.
5. A strike is called for each foul tip.
6. The batter is out on a third strike, including an uncaught foul ball.
7. A player may lead off from base with a risk of being picked off, but may not advance on a resultant overthrow.
8. The ball is in play on a ball or strike, including the third strike.

GAME PLAY FOR BEGINNERS OR CHILDREN

In teaching softball to children and unskilled players, it may be desirable to modify the official rules for purposes of player enjoyment. The following rule adaptations are suggested for consideration in teaching a beginning softball class:[2]

1. Softer balls may be substituted for the regulation 12-inch softball. In addition, slower flight balls and super-soft softballs allow defensive players additional time to make plays and deters

---

[1] American Alliance for Health, Physical Education, and Recreation, *NAGWS Softball Guide* (Washington, D.C.: AAHPER, 1979-1981), p. 81.
[2] American Alliance for Health, Physical Education and Recreation, *NAGWS Softball Guide* (Washington, D.C.: AAHPER, 1977-1979), p. 98.

player fear of injury when catching a hard hit ball. A 16-inch ball may be used, when space is limited.

2. The diamond dimensions may be altered to include:
   a. Lengthening the baselines from 45 to 55 feet, which allows an unskilled defensive player more time to successfully complete outs.
   b. Increasing the distance between home plate and the pitcher's plate for safety reasons and to increase the pitcher's potential as a fielder.
3. Only slow-pitch pitching is allowed.
4. Players may steal second or third, but to avoid any collisions or dangerous plays at the plate, they may not steal home.
5. Despite the location of a ball in foul territory, only one base on an overthrow is allowed.
6. Regardless of how the catcher handles the pitch, a batter is declared automatically out on the third strike.
7. The infield fly rule is optional.

PROJECTS FOR THE PROSPECTIVE TEACHER/COACH

1. Devise a lead-up or novelty game and teach it to a class of beginning players or prospective teachers.
2. Organize and conduct a co-recreational game using adapted rules in a class or recreational setting under the supervision of an instructor.

Evaluation

In an educational setting, evaluation of psychomotor and cognitive competencies should be an integral part of the teaching process. Most evaluative procedures only measure the performance at the time of testing and not potential performance. Therefore periodic evaluation is desirable in determining the student's progression and improvement. Repeated evaluations may also serve as practice sessions and motivational devices, thus making instruction more meaningful. Pretests are valuable in obtaining basic information for later comparisons. To determine improvement, periodic or post-unit tests render feedback regarding instructional effectiveness.

Various measurement techniques may be employed to determine a player's success in meeting desired personal and group objectives. To evaluate skill and knowledge levels, three appropriate instruments—skill tests, rating scales, and knowledge tests—are frequently applied. In selecting tests suitable for evaluating performance in a given situation, several criteria should be considered, such as validity, reliability, scoring method, degree of difficulty, and administrative feasibility. The authors recommend the following tests for skill assessment.

SKILL TESTS

The American Alliance for Health, Physical Education, Recreation and Dance endorsed eight comprehensive tests of softball skills and provided national performance norms for ages 10 to 18. Seven of these tests appear below. Based upon the twentieth percentile scores for each age group and sex, a performance expectancy chart has been designed to accompany these tests (Table 8.1). Performance scores charted for ages 7 to 12 provide minimal acceptable expectations for beginning level players. Expectations for 13 to 15-year-olds suggest minimal, intermediate level skill standards. Scores for the age range of 16 to 18 offer lower limit expectations for the advanced level players.

Regarding the administration of these tests, student assistants may be trained in the techniques of testing when employing a station-to-station procedure.

1. **Throw for distance.** Measures the distance a softball can be thrown (Fig. 8.1).
   Equipment. A smooth grass or dirt field with throwing-zone lines marked (five-yard lines marked if possible), softballs, measuring tape, and stake markers.
   Description. Mark off a zone six feet wide from which the throw must be made. One or two steps may be taken preceding the throw. The player throws three balls at right angles to the

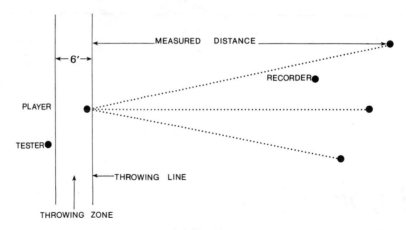

Figure 8.1
Throw for distance

throwing line. Mark the point at which the first ball hits the ground. If the second or third throw is farther, mark the new point. It speeds up measuring if, after three consecutive throws, the player stands at the furthest mark. After four or five players have thrown, all their distances can be measured at the same time. Players must be warmed up before throwing. Throws must be measured at right angles to the throwing line and to the nearest measured foot. (This test is the same as the softball throw in the AAHPER Youth Fitness Test Manual.) The distance of the best throw should be recorded on the squad scorecard.

2. **Overhand throw for accuracy.** Measures the accuracy of a throw from the approximate distance of an infielder's throw to a base or home plate (Fig. 8.2).

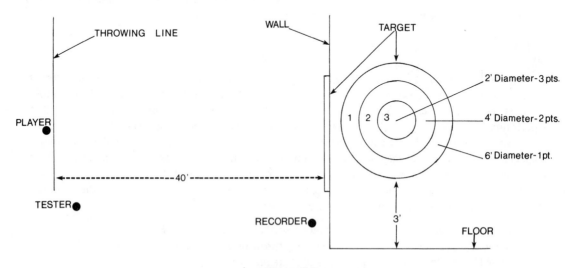

Figure 8.2
Overhand throw for accuracy

Equipment. A smooth wall on which a target can be placed, or a target marked on the wall; softballs, measuring tape, chalk.

Description. The target consists of three concentric circles, marked by lines one inch wide, painted on an area at least eight feet square. A wall, or a canvas or mat hung on the wall, may be used. The center circle is two feet in diameter, and the outer circle six feet in diameter. The bottom of the outer circle is three feet above the floor. The throw is made from behind a line parallel to, and 65 feet from, the target. After one or two practice throws, the player throws ten times. Both feet must be behind the line at the time of the throw, but the player may take one or two steps before making the throw.

Scoring. Balls hitting in the center circle count three points; in the middle area, count two points; and in the outer area count one point. Balls hitting on a line count as the higher number of points. The score is the sum of points made on ten throws. Record points as each throw is made. The maximum score is 30 points.

3. **Underhand pitching.** Measures the accuracy with which a softball can be pitched. (Fig. 8.3).

Equipment. A gymnasium or outdoor space adjacent to a smooth wall, target, softballs, measuring tape, chalk.

Description. A rectangular target with an inner rectangle 17 inches wide and 30 inches high, and an outer rectangle which is six inches larger on all sides, is painted on canvas or marked on a wall. The lines are one inch wide. The target is placed so that the bottom of the outer rectangle is 18 inches above the floor. A pitching line 24 inches long is marked 46 feet from the target and parallel to it. The player is allowed one practice pitch and then takes 15 underhand pitches.

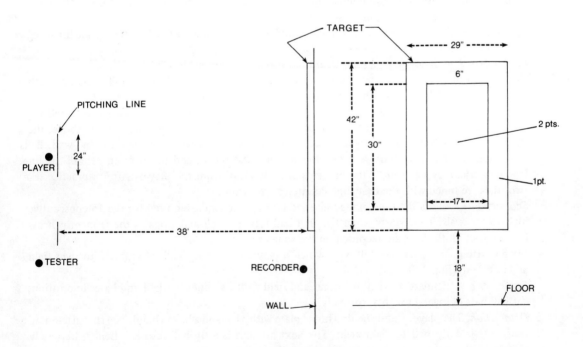

Figure 8.3
Underhand pitching

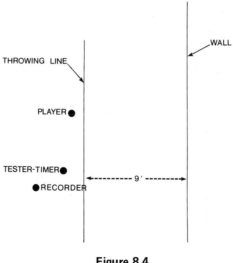

Figure 8.4
Speed throw

One foot must be kept on the pitching line while delivering the ball. A forward step can be taken while making the pitch. Illegal pitches should not be scored.

Scoring. Pitched balls hitting in the center area, or on its boundary line, count two points; in the outer area, or on its outside boundary line, count one point. The score is the sum of all points made on 15 pitches. The maximum score is 30 points.

4. **Speed throw.** Measures the speed with which a player can handle the ball in catching and throwing (Fig. 8.4).

Equipment. A gymnasium or a smooth ground surface, softballs, stopwatch.

Description. A line is drawn on the floor or ground, nine feet from, and parallel to, a smooth wall eight to ten feet in width and height. From behind the line, the player throws the ball overhand against the wall, and catches the rebound as rapidly as possible. This is repeated for 15 throws. For best results, the ball should hit the wall at the height of, or a bit above, the thrower. Players start on the signal "go," but time is started when the ball hits the wall. Balls which fall short can be retrieved, but the player must return and throw from behind the line. One new trial may be given if the ball gets entirely away from the player. After a practice trial, two trials are timed with the best time counted as the score.

Scoring. The score is the time in seconds, and tenths of seconds, required for the 15 consecutive hits on the wall. Time starts when the first ball hits the wall and stops as the fifteenth throw hits the wall. Both times are recorded on the squad scorecard.

5. **Fungo hitting.** Measures the skill with which a player can hit fly balls alternately to right field and left field. (Fig. 8.5).

Equipment. A standard softball diamond and field with baselines marked and bases in position; softball bats of several weights, softballs.

Description. The player stands behind home plate with a bat and a ball in hand. The first attempted fungo hit is a fly ball to right field. The next attempt is a fly ball into left field. Alternately hitting to the right and left is continued until ten hits are attempted to each side (a total of 20 hits). The score is recorded as each ball is hit and the sums of the 20 hits are counted as the

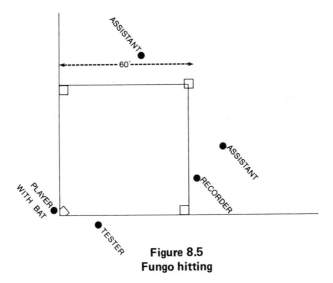

Figure 8.5
Fungo hitting

score. Two balls missed entirely, in succession, count as an attempt. The tester may call "right" or "left" to indicate the side to which the next hit is to be hit. Practice trials to each side are allowed. *Scoring.* Fly balls which land beyond the baseline on the intended side count two points, while ground balls hit across the baseline on the intended side count one point. Foul balls and balls settling in the infield count zero points. When hits intended for right field land at the left of second base, no score is made. Similarly when balls intended for left field go to the right of second base, no score is made. The maximum score is 40 points.

6. **Baserunning.** Measures the speed with which a player can run around the bases after a swing at an imaginary pitch (Fig. 8.6).
   Equipment. A standard softball field and diamond with home plate, bases, and a batter's box laid out for a right-handed batter; softball bats, stopwatch.
   Description. The player takes position in the right-hand batter's box, holding a bat as if ready for a pitch. On the signal "hit" the player takes a complete swing at an imaginary ball, drops the bat (it must not be thrown), and runs around the bases, being careful to touch each base. A practice run is allowed. Two trials are recorded and the best score is counted. The trials are timed in seconds and tenths of seconds from the signal "hit," to the instant the runner touches home plate after circling the bases.

7. **Fielding ground balls.** Measures the ability of a player to field ground balls quickly (Fig. 8.7).
   Equipment. A smooth area on which markings can be placed, softballs, baskets, a sweep-hand watch, measuring tape, marking equipment (lime, tapes, or trenches).
   Description. An area 17 by 60 feet is marked on a field. A throwing line is designated at one end. Two lines are drawn in this area, a line 50 feet from the throwing line and the other 25 feet from the throwing line. The player being tested stands inside the ten-foot area beyond the 50-foot line. An assistant with the basket of ten balls stands behind the throwing line. Spare balls are available if needed. On signal "go," the assistant throws grounders into the marked area at five-second intervals. Each throw must strike the ground, for at least one bounce, between the throwing line and the 25-foot line and be within the side lines. The thrower should throw overhand with good

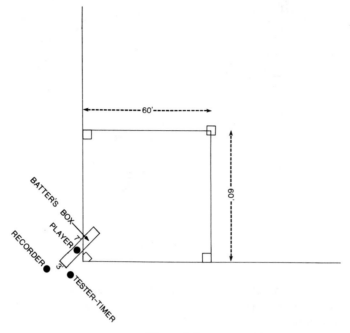

Figure 8.6
Baserunning

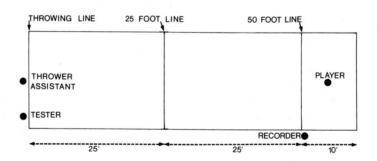

Figure 8.7
Fielding ground balls

speed, like a machine, with some variation in direction, but not trying to make the fielder miss. A throw not made as specified can be repeated. The player must field each ball cleanly, hold it momentarily, toss it aside, and then prepare for the next ball. The player starts behind the 50-foot line but thereafter fields anywhere behind the 25-foot line. If a series of throws is interrupted, it may be repeated at the discretion of the tester. A practice trial is allowed.

Scoring. Each ball correctly fielded counts one point. Record a point or a zero for each throw. The score is the total of points on 20 throws; the maximum score is 20 points.

Table 8.1
Minimal Skill Performance Expectancy
(By age group and sex)

Test	7-9	10-12	13-15	16-18
Males				
Throw for distance	49 ft.	91 ft.	133 ft.	161 ft.
Overhand throw for accuracy	1 pt.	2 pts.	6 pts.	8 pts.
Underhand pitching	1 pt.	2 pts.	4 pts.	5 pts.
Speed throw	30 sec.	25.3 sec.	20.2 sec.	18.8 sec.
Fungo hitting	not suitable	11 pts.	15 pts.	16 pts.
Baserunning	17.9 sec.	16.2 sec.	14.5 sec.	13.6 sec.
Fielding ground balls	9 pts.	10 pts.	10 pts.	11 pts.
Females				
Throw for distance	31	46	61	62
Overhand throw for accuracy	1 pt.	2 pts.	4 pts.	5 pts.
Underhand pitching	1 pt.	1 pt.	3 pts.	5 pts.
Speed throw	41.5 sec.	34.7 sec.	27.9 sec.	25.9 sec.
Fungo hitting	not suitable	5 pts.	9 pts.	11 pts.
Baserunning	18 sec.	17.1 sec.	16.2 sec.	16.7 sec.
Fielding ground balls	5 pts.	8 pts.	11 pts.	14 pts.

Based on National Norms at the twentieth percentile level for each test. Estimates were made in determining minimal group expectations.

8. **Catching fly balls.** Measures skill in catching at frequent intervals (Fig. 8.8). In testing beginners, the balls should be thrown. However, for intermediate and advanced players the balls may be thrown or batted.

   Description. The student being tested stands approximately 60 feet from the tosser who has a ball in hand and a supply of balls within reach. On the signal "go" given by the tester, the tosser makes overhand throws of approximately 30 feet in height to the player. The player must catch each ball and then toss or roll it to a catcher standing beside the tosser. The tosser continues

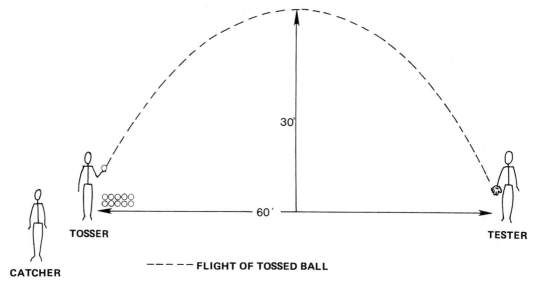

Figure 8.8
Catching fly balls

to throw at ten-second intervals. The tester can time the throws if necessary. Two trials of ten throws each are taken. The score is the number of balls successfully caught of the 20 thrown. Suggested minimal skill performances are as follows:

Age	Males	Females
7- 9	13	5
10-12	14	7
13-15	15	9
16-18	17	13

9. **Repeated throws.**[1] Measures a player's ability to catch an aerial ball and make a rapid throw (Fig. 8.9). This is similar to the test for *fielding ground balls.* A restraining line is drawn 23 feet from a smooth wall, and a line is drawn on the wall ten feet from the floor and parallel to it. *Description.* The player stands behind the restraining line, facing the wall, with a ball in the throwing hand. On the signal "go," the player throws the ball overhand or sidearm at the wall, so that it strikes above the ten-foot line, and then catches the return as it comes off the wall. The player repeats the process as rapidly as possible. Each throw must be made from behind the 23-foot line. Any mishandled ball must be recovered before the next throw. A practice trial precedes each of the four 30-second trials. For each ball that is thrown from behind the 23-foot line and strikes the wall above the ten-foot line, a point is scored. Points totalled for all four trials. Suggested minimal skill performances are as follows:

[1] Jacqueline Shick, "Battery of Defensive Softball Skills Tests," *Softball Guide, January 1972-1974,* (Washington, D.C.: AAHPER, 1972), p. 61. Reprinted by permission of the American Alliance for Health, Physical Education, and Recreation, Washington, D.C.

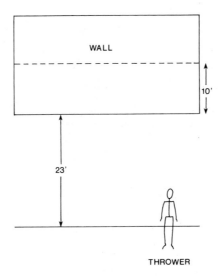

Figure 8.9
Repeated throws

Age	Males	Females
7- 9	20	17
10-12	24	20
13-15	30	24
16-18	40	30

10. **The batting tee test.**[2] Suitable for assessing the beginners' ability to hit squarely a stationary ball for distance. (Figure 8.10). (Batting form may be subjectively evaluated while testing.) In preparation for the test, mark off 15 parallel lines, each five yards apart on an open playing area. A batting tee is placed in the middle of the first line.

    Description. The batter assumes a normal batting stance and hits a ball off the tee as far as possible. Five practice trials are allowed, followed by 20 trials for score. (The authors suggest that in evaluating a large class, the number of trials may be reduced if time is limited.) The distance is measured to the nearest yard from the tee to the point where each ball first lands. The recorded score is a total of the distances for the 20 trials. Presently norms are not available as indicators of minimal skill performances.

11. **Batting pitched balls.**[3] Recommended as one instrument for determining a player's ability to hit a pitched ball into fair territory (Fig. 8.11). Unless a pitching machine is used to provide uniformity in every pitch, the teacher must recognize the possibility of a loss of reliability in the test. However, when using a player for pitching purposes, it is suggested to have the same pitcher throw similar pitches to all tested players. Another alternative is to use two pitchers, administer the test twice, and total both scores.

---

[2] Dorothy Mohr, "Skill Testing," *Softball Guide, January 1962-1964,* (Washington, D.C.: AAHPER, 1962), pp. 45-56. Reprinted by permission of the American Alliance for Health, Physical Education, and Recreation, Washington, D.C.
[3] *Ibid.,* p. 46.

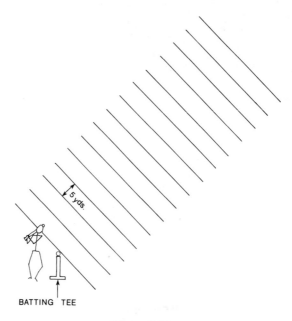

Figure 8.10
Batting tee test

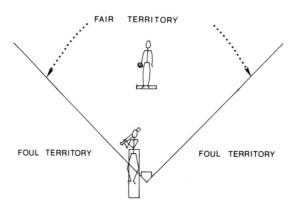

Figure 8.11
Batting pitched balls

Description. The batter stands in the batter's box and is allowed ten trials to hit legal underhand pitches. Strikes may be called by an umpire, if desired, but balls are disregarded. Three points are awarded for balls hit into fair territory, one point is awarded for a foul ball, and no points for strikes (called or missed). The total points for the ten trials are recorded.

The authors choose not to recommend minimal skill performances for this test due to variations in pitches and differences in hitting slow vs. fast pitched balls. Each instructor is encouraged to establish standards suitable for the situation and skill level of the players involved.

RATING SCALES AND CHECKLISTS

Observation of players in practice and game situations is vital in assessing skill technique. Rating scales and checklists contribute objectivity to these observational appraisals. Such lists categorize offensive and defensive skills into their basic components. Furthermore, rating scales allow the observer to designate the level of proficiency in executing each skill. The following checklist may be adapted to any level of play by adding relevant skills. For example, if assessing beginning skill and strategy execution, the instructor would evaluate pitching, base covering, backing up double plays, sacrifice plays, and relays. For advanced players, the addition of place hitting, bunting, hit-and-run, and base stealing would be appropriate.

Table 8.2
Checklist for Rating Fundamental Softball Skills
(Rate player's form for each skill component:
3 = excellent, 2 = good, 1 = fair, 0 = poor)

Skill	Excellent	Good	Fair	Poor
Throwing				
Grip				
Focus on target				
Footwork				
Weight shift				
Body rotation				
Arm motion and release				
Follow-through				
Total				
Catching				
Focus on ball				
Body position (relative to ball)				
Footwork				
Glove or hand position				
Watching ball into glove				
"Giving" with ball				
Total				

Table 8.2—*Continued*

Skill	Excellent	Good	Fair	Poor
Batting				
Grip				
Focus on ball				
Stance				
Bat position				
Stride				
Swing				
Point of contact with ball				
Follow-through				
Total				
Fielding				
Body position (relative to ball)				
Handling ground balls				
Footwork				
Focus on target				
Arm motion and quick release				
Follow-through				
Total				
Baserunning				
Leaving the batter's box				
Sprint down the line				
Approach to the base				
Tagging the base				
Rounding the base				
Safely stopping on a base				
Overrunning 1st base and home				
Total				

Table 8.2—*Continued*

Skill	Excellent	Good	Fair	Poor
Pitching				
Focus on target				
Stance				
Backswing				
Delivery				
Follow-through				
Assuming fielding position				
Total				
Overall Total				

OTHER PERFORMANCE ASSESSMENT TECHNIQUES

Game statistics may offer the instructor valuable information regarding a student's application of game skills. In assessing the player's "total" skill performance, consideration should be given to several individual statistics, including batting averages, errors, stolen bases, strikeouts, sacrifice flies, bases on balls, etc. As the skill level of the class increases, statistical information can be used to a greater extent for evaluative purposes. Students should be familiarized with each statistical category as the corresponding rules are introduced.

Proper scorekeeping techniques can be taught and practiced in class. Players unable to actively participate may be involved in the game as scorers and statisticians.

WRITTEN TESTS

In addition to reports and class discussions, student achievement of the cognitive objectives for the softball unit may be objectively determined through the use of written quizzes and examinations. Knowledge tests should reflect the cognitive competencies desired for all players of that level. Ambiguous questions which allow for variances of interpretation should be eliminated. Well-constructed, teacher-made tests may be more relevant and suitable to the situation than standardized tests.

The content of each examination should correspond to the knowledge and skill progressions taught. As in skill assessment, the difficulty of cognitive examinations will increase with the experience of the students. Listed below are suggested contents for the beginning and advanced-level examinations. The applicable rules can be found in three popular rule guides published by the National Association of Girls and Women's Sports, the National Federation of High School Athletic Associations, and the Amateur Softball Association.

Beginning Level Content

1. History and value of game
2. Safety and sportsmanship
3. Facilities and equipment
4. Terminology
5. Rules
   a. Strikes and balls
   b. Fair and foul balls
   c. Overthrows
   d. Leaving base too soon
   e. Overrunning bases
   f. Missing a base
   g. Running out of a baseline
   h. Two people on a base
   i. Hit by a ball
   j. Regulation inning and game
   k. Legally caught ball
   l. Double plays
   m. Pitching
   n. Batting
6. Strategy
   a. Relay
   b. Positioning fielders
   c. Covering
   d. Backing up
   e. Sacrifice fly
7. Fundamentals of beginning skills

Advanced Level Content

1. New Terminology
2. Rules
   a. Coach's interference
   b. Obstruction and interference
   c. Advanced baserunning rules
   d. Advanced pitching regulations
   e. Bunting
   f. Infield fly
   g. Catcher interference
   h. Ground rules
   i. Sacrifice fly
   j. Third strike rule
   k. Passed ball
   l. Appeal plays
3. Scorekeeping technique
4. Strategy
   a. Place hitting
   b. Pitching
   c. Covering
   d. Backing up
   e. Sacrifice bunt
   f. Hit and run
   g. Squeeze play
   h. Stealing
5. Base coaching
6. Fundamentals of advanced skills
7. Officiating

PROJECTS FOR THE PROSPECTIVE TEACHER/COACH

1. Request from a local softball instructor his/her evaluative procedures used for determining student programs and grades.
2. Devise a written test on softball rules, skills, and strategies consisting of multiple choice, true and false, and short answer questions.
3. Devise a crossword puzzle utilizing softball terminology.
4. Assist a teacher or coach in administering skill tests.
5. Research additional skill tests and evaluate the strengths and weaknesses of each.

Coaching Competitive Softball

This chapter discusses the responsibilities of a softball coach—administrative duties, organizational techniques—and presents suggestions for practice and games to assist the beginning coach.

PRE-SEASON RESPONSIBILITIES

Scheduling. Ideally, the scheduling of interscholastic games should be initiated at the completion of the previous season and finalized well in advance of the first game. This allows time for transportation, budgetary, and facility arrangements. Consideration should be given to scheduling easier competition for games early in the season, thus allowing the team sufficient time to prepare for major competition. In recreation leagues, a director prepares and issues the schedule to all teams. However, the coach may schedule additional invitational tournaments or practice games.

Contracting. Contracts should be signed by the teams involved to bind the agreement.

Obtaining travel permits. Travel permits should be signed by the parents or guardians of all minors for away and overnight trips. Although such permits do not relegate the coach's or school's liability, obtaining parental consent is a courtesy that promotes a cooperative effort between the parents and coaches.

Budgeting. Each spring, interscholastic budgetary requests must be submitted by the coach to the athletic director. Requests should be based upon program needs, which are assessed through an accurate inventory, a tentative schedule of games, and budgetary expenditures during the past five years. The coach must consider the expenses which will be incurred for transportation, officials, uniforms, laundry service, equipment and supplies, maintenance, lights, and field rental and improvements. Estimated receipts may include fund raising activities, donations, admission fees, and school allocations.

Procuring officials. Quality officials may be available through the local officiating board, or will be assigned by the league or conference director.

Transporting players. For safety and liability purposes, interscholastic players should be transported by a school bus or van, as opposed to personal cars. It is strongly recommended and sometimes required that the driver possesses a certified chauffeur's license.

Ordering. Once the budget has been approved, equipment and uniforms should be ordered promptly. Orders with specifications that deviate from standard, in-stock items require additional time for manufacturing.

Selecting a team. Although budgetary and philosophical considerations affect the coach's decision regarding the number of players on the team, it is important to have several utility players. Ideally, each utility player can serve as a back up for more than one position. For competitive fast-pitch play, it is desirable to have three pitchers and three catchers due to the strenuous nature and importance of these positions. Slow-pitch play may require fewer back ups in these positions. In selecting players certain personal qualities in athletes are desirable, such as self-discipline on and off the field, the motivation to excel, and a proper competitive attitude. The team's probability of success may be enhanced by the selection of players who are team-oriented, unselfish, supportive, and respectful of others.

Conducting tryouts. A one- to two-week period for tryouts will allow the coach sufficient time to assess each player's potential. Former varsity players should be expected to try out with other candidates. No player should be guaranteed a position on the squad without meeting the established criteria for that particular season. Running, stretching exercises, ball handling warm-ups, infield and outfield drills, batting practice, baserunning techniques, and game play should be integrated in the tryout sessions.

Meeting with the team. At the initial team meeting the coach, either directly or indirectly, shares the staff's coaching philosophy with the players. In turn, players may be requested to reflect on their personal team goals and expectations for the season. Players should be encouraged to share their ideas and maintain an open line of communication as a team, but must realize that all final decisions rest with the coach. The humanistic coach knows that players who strive for and attain realistic goals may have improved self-images, self-awareness, and a better team concept.

The coach must be certain every player is knowledgeable of the coach's expectations for the season. Training rules and eligibility regulations must be understood by all concerned, including the parents. Policy information should be disseminated to guardians of all players through a letter from the coach or parental attendance at team meetings. Players must be knowledgeable of proper diet, sleeping, and study habits. Frequently, a dedicated athlete will become so involved in athletics that academics are no longer valued. It is the coach's responsibility to integrate athletics with the total school experience.

Building good public relations. Sound public relations can result in good community support for the team. Once the team is selected, the coach should prepare information for the media on returning players, new prospects, and the season's schedule. Sportscasters and sportswriters of local and school newspapers may be contacted for possible coverage during the season.

On away games, the scorekeeper or manager can be delegated, immediately after each game, the responsibility of furnishing game results to newspapers and radio and television stations. In addition, local newspapers frequently run a daily section on high school sports, including an Athlete of the Week article. Outstanding athletes or performances should be brought to the sportswriters' attention.

The coach may arouse community interest through talks to civic groups, by organizing team projects which serve the community, and by initiating an active softball booster organization.

RESPONSIBILITIES DURING THE COMPETITIVE SEASON

Mentally Preparing the Team

During the competitive season the coach is faced with the task of mentally preparing the team for each game. Generally, however, there is no problem in generating enthusiasm at the beginning of the season or against rival schools. In mentally preparing a team, the coach must stress the team concept, the importance of each game, the value of giving 100 percent effort at all times, and proper respect for the abilities of opponents and teammates.

A team may meet prior to a game and share realistic team objectives and strategies for the contest. Caution must be taken not to assert undue pressure on the players to win, through negative reinforcement.

At practice on the day following a game, techniques or strategies which were faulty should be analyzed and improved upon. Viewing films of the game may be extremely helpful in this analysis. Once the highlights and mistakes of the previous game have been discussed, it becomes past history and every team member should concentrate on preparing for the next game.

Conducting Practice Sessions

During the practice sessions, the coach must analyze player skills, and offer kinesthetic explanations for faulty performance in terms understood by the players. The key to successful coaching is the ability to capitalize on the strengths and compensate for the weaknesses of individual players. Once the coach analyzes each player's performance, the necessary adjustments may be made for competitive play. For example, a player with inadequate batting skills but strong fielding ability may play a key position on the field yet bat in a less demanding position in the batting order. Conversely, a strong batter but poor fielder could be a designated hitter.

Daily practice sessions should be mentally and physically challenging and include calisthenics, warm-ups, infield and outfield practice, baserunning, and batting practice. Specific days should be devoted to rundowns, relays and cutoffs, squeeze plays, and other offensive and defensive strategies. Drills need to be as game-like as possible. Once the season begins, a team should spend little time scrimmaging.

Each practice should start with stretching exercises. When properly warmed up, an athlete may be less likely to sustain strains and sprains in the muscles, tendons, and ligaments. The range of motion in the joints is increased, and coordination is improved. After players have warmed up sufficiently, they will need to go through a series of drills to warm up their throwing arms. The practice can then continue with drills necessary to prepare the team for the next game.

The sample practice schedule (Table 9.1) gives a basic plan for organizing practices. Drills should progress from simple to complex. It is important to vary practices to keep players alert mentally and challenged physically.

A practice schedule, similar to the one cited, may keep the team active for approximately two hours. Practices of longer duration may be ineffective.

Staffing

An integral part of a softball team is the coach's supporting staff. Few schools hire an assistant coach. However, knowledgeable parents, community members, former players, or university students may be interested in donating time in order to gain coaching experience.

A qualified scorekeeper and team statistician are necessary to keep accurate records. Such records assist the coach in planning practices and in strategically playing the team members. Additionally, the coach who has accurate statistics on players can assist the scouted athletes desiring college scholarships.

The team manager is responsible for securing eligibility slips, caring for equipment, and having the field lined off before each game. The manager also attends all practices and games, and assists in any capacity deemed necessary by the coach.

Table 9.1
Sample Practice Schedule

15 minutes	Stretches, jog two laps, monkey slides.
15 minutes	Shuttle grounders, shuttle flies, throwing relays with teams of three; players 60 feet apart.

30 minutes   Infield
1. Continuous catches: each infielder stops ten consecutively hit ground balls.
2. Continuous throws: each infielder stops ten consecutively hit ground balls and makes an accurate throw to first on each ball.
3. Double play combinations with other infielders as baserunners. Run through each combination three times: 2-ss-1, 3-2-1, ss-2-1, 1-2-ss.

Outfield
1. Standing in single-line formation, players field easily hit balls to their right and left. Follow the same procedure with more difficult balls.
2. Back to batter: each outfielder stands with back to the batter. On signal "take it," the fielder turns to face the hit ball, calls for it and catches the fly. Rotate through each fielder three times.
3. Players form two lines. Ball is hit between the two lines and fielders either call for the ball or back up the other player. Players change lines after fielding the ball.
4. Follow the same procedure as 3 above, but with three lines.

5 minutes   Water break.

25 minutes   Batting practice
Four players to a group (pitcher, batter, and two fielders). Each player bats until coach gives signal to rotate.

5 minutes   Baserunning sprints
1. Sprint to first, jog to second, sprint to third, jog home.
2. Sprint to second, jog to third, sprint home.
3. Sprint to third, jog home.
4. Sprint around the horn.

5 minutes   Water break.

20 minutes   Scrimmage (outfielders vs. infielders)
Each team is comprised of seven to ten players. The teams may decide the field positions for their players. The team at bat must have at least two players on base every inning or run one rabbit drill before going into the field.

5 minutes   Baserunner suicide (see Chapter 6).

Adapted from Sue Whiddon and Suzanne Robinson, "Responsibilities of the Softball Coach Before and During the Competitive Season," *Women's Coaching Clinic* 2 (April, 1979):13.

It is not always possible for a team physician to be at every game. However, a physician should be on-call in the event of a serious injury. It is strongly recommended that a trainer attend all practices and games. In addition, students who have successfully completed a first aid course, or preferably the Cramer Student Trainer Course, may be valuable assets to any athletic team and athletic trainer.

Conducting Warm-ups

Proper selection and use of warm-up drills is very important to effective team play. Warm-up drills may have a psychological as well as physiological effect on a team. Players often need the opportunity to warm up muscles and become conditioned to the field environment. In addition, a well planned and executed drill can boost a team's confidence and offer an impressive display of player skill and team organization. The pre-game and pre-inning warm-ups in this chapter may be used as presented, or may be modified for use with different skill levels.

Pre-game Batting Practice

Approximately one hour prior to game time, each player should be allowed ten to 15 warm-up hits. When the field must be shared, the home team practices in left field and the visitors in right field, with batters assuming positions along the third and first base lines respectively. Fielders assume scattered positions in the field and rotate clockwise to become the batter. To expedite the process, the right fielder should rotate to an on-deck position. During the first few hits the batter should be concerned primarily with making contact and executing a fluid swing. Subsequent attempts should receive place hitting emphasis.

Pre-game Infield Warm-up

The coach fungo hits to infielders in the following suggested sequence:

1. A ground ball is hit to third base. The third baseman throws to first base. The first baseman returns the ball to third. The ball is then thrown from second, to first, and to the catcher.
2. A ground ball is hit to the shortstop. The shortstop throws the ball to first. The first baseman throws to the shortstop covering second. The ball is thrown from second to first to the catcher.
3. A ground ball is hit to the second baseman. The throw is made to first base. The first baseman returns the ball to the second baseman covering the base. The ball is thrown from second to first to the catcher.
4. A ground ball is hit to the first baseman, who tosses to the second baseman covering first. The ball is thrown to the catcher and returned to the first baseman covering the bag. The first baseman throws to the catcher.
5. A ball is bunted a short distance in front of home plate. The catcher fields the ball and throws to first. The first baseman throws back to the catcher covering home.
6. A ground ball is hit to each infielder who tags or throws to the closest bag and completes one of the following double plays: second to first, third to second, first to third, home to second.

Pre-game Outfield Warm-up

While infielders are warming up the following outfield drill should be conducted. A batter standing on the outfield foul line fungo hits balls to players in a shuttle-line formation. In turn, each player catches the ball and returns it to a catcher beside the fungo batter and takes a position at the end of the line.

Toward the end of the infielder's practice time, the starting outfielders take their respective positions on the field and participate in the following drills which complete their warm-up.

1. A fly ball is hit respectively to the left, center, and right fielders. The fielders return the ball to the catcher on the first bounce.
2. A fly ball is hit to left and center fielders. The fielders throw to second baseman covering second. The ball is relayed from second, to first, to the catcher.
3. A ground ball is hit to each infielder. The infielder throws the ball to the catcher and charges toward home. The catcher then rolls a second ball back to the charging player. The second ball fielded is tossed easily to the catcher, and the player continues off the field. Outfielders are hit short balls. Each fielder catches the ball, throws it to the catcher and runs off the field.

Pre-inning Warm-up

As the pitcher warms up by pitching the legal number of pitches to the catcher, the first baseman throws ground balls to the third baseman, shortstop, and second baseman. Each infielder fields the ball and throws to the first baseman. The outfielders take their positions in the field and practice throwing in relay formation to one another. The left fielder throws to the short fielder, the short fielder to the center fielder, the center fielder to the right fielder. The process is then repeated in reverse order. If the defensive team's bench is on the first base line the right fielder assumes responsibility for starting the warm-up. An alternative slow-pitch warm-up involves the left fielder and center field throwing to each other, while the short fielder and right fielder do likewise.

Determining the Lineup

Prior to the game the coach should develop the lineup based upon players' performances and attitudes in recent games and practices. There are varying theories on whether strong hitters should be staggered in the lineup or stacked at the beginning. A coach must be aware that players at the beginning of the lineup have more times at bat. Standard procedure dictates the first batter should be a good hitter and baserunner. In addition, this batter should be able to judge balls and strikes accurately and get on base. Ideally, the second batter would be left-handed and capable of hitting behind a runner. The team's best hitters will be third and fifth in the order, with a long-ball hitter batting fourth. The next best hitter bats sixth. The seventh hitter is frequently the second-best leadoff batter, capable of getting on base. The last few batters should have sufficient bunting ability to advance any runners. Coaches should be familiar with the current designated hitter and reentry rules when determining the strongest possible lineup.

Base Coaching

Offensive signals need to be developed by the batter and coach. Players should give a signal as they approach the plate to indicate to the coach: "I'm ready to watch the ball meet the bat." The coach should have signals to indicate such cues as: "Take it," "Go left," "Go right," "Up the middle," "Hit away."

Players must have faith in the base coaches' judgments and obey signals without hesitation. As soon as the ball is hit, the batter becomes a baserunner, and should be looking directly at the first base coach. The first base coach will let the runner know whether to overrun the bag or make a turn toward second. As a runner nears second base, eye contact must be made with the third base coach. The coach will indicate whether to slide, hold up, or continue running to third. When the runner comes toward third, the coach will again indicate what the baserunner should do.

Throughout the game, and at its conclusion, coaches and players should display good sportsmanship. Win or lose, a congratulatory gesture in the form of a handshaking line communicates the players appreciation for the opposing team.

PROJECTS FOR THE PROSPECTIVE COACH

1. Visit a local team and observe their practice procedures for a day. Discuss and compare their procedures with those observed by your classmates.
2. Observe a softball game and keep scouting statistics on each team.
3. Obtain catalogue information on uniforms made by different companies, and compare for price and suitability. Submit a written report of your findings.
4. Volunteer to assist coaches in community softball programs. Log your experiences and submit it to your instructor.
5. Design team warm-up procedures for a game. Using your classmates as players, implement your warm-ups at the beginning of a class session.
6. Write your own philosophy of coaching.

Appendix

	Fast Pitch	Slow Pitch
Players	A team shall consist of nine players.	A team shall consist of ten players.
Bunting or Chopping	Legal	Illegal
Base stealing or lead-off	Baserunners may lead off or steal on the pitch, as soon as the ball leaves the pitcher's hand.	Stealing is not allowed. Runners may leave their bases when a pitched ball has reached or crossed home plate, or is hit.
Pitching	The pitch is delivered with an underhand motion with both feet in contact with the pitcher's plate. One step forward is allowed, it must be toward the batter and simultaneous with the delivery of the ball to the batter.	The pitch is delivered with an underhand motion at a moderate speed with a perceptible arch not over 12 feet in height. One foot must be in contact with the pitcher's plate during the delivery. If a step is taken, it must be toward home plate.
Illegal pitch	A ball is called on the batter and all baserunners are awarded one base.	A ball is called on the batter and runners do not advance.
Pitching irregularities, dropping the ball from the pitcher's hand	If the ball slips from the pitcher's hand during his wind-up or during the backswing, the ball is in play and runners may advance with the liability to be put out.	A "no pitch" is called. The ball is dead and any subsequent action is cancelled.
Strike zone	Area between the batter's arm pits and the top of the knees during natural batting stance.	No higher than the batter's highest shoulder and no lower than the knees during natural batting stance.

Foul tip	A strike is called and the ball is in play.	A strike is called and the ball is dead.
Foul line distances	For men and women, the minimum foul line distance is 225 feet.	For women, the minimum foul line distance is 250 feet. For men, the minimum foul line is 275 feet.
Intentional walk	The pitcher must throw four pitches outside the strike zone. The ball is in play.	The team notifies the umpire who awards the batter first base. The ball is dead.
Ball four	Base is awarded and the ball is in play.	Base is awarded and the ball is dead.
Advancing on a passed ball	Players may advance on a passed ball with liability to be put out.	Player may not advance on passed ball. The ball is dead.
Designated hitter	Legal	Illegal
Third strike rule	Ball is in play after the third strike and batter becomes a baserunner with liability to be put out. With two outs and a runner on first the batter is out.	Batter is out.

Glossary

Backing up. A fielder moving behind another fielder to stop the ball in case of error.

Ball. A pitch which is not in the strike zone of a batter.

Battery. The pitcher and catcher on the defensive team.

Bunt. A ball tapped a short distance down either foul line, or in front of home plate, by a batter attempting to advance a baserunner or achieve an infield hit.

Covering the base. Assuming a baseman's position and responsibility when a putout could be made at the base.

Choking up. A "short" grip. Moving the hands up the bat for better control in hitting.

Cutoff. An infielder's interception of a throw from an outfielder or another infielder when no play can be made at the intended base, or when another play is foreseen.

Dominant hand. The hand that is preferred for throwing.

Double play. A defensive manuever resulting in two outs in one play.

Drag bunt. Without taking a bunting stance, the batter lowers the bat to contact the ball and attempts to beat the throw to first base for a hit. The drag bunt is usually executed down the first base line by left-handed batters and down the third base line by right-handed batters.

Error. A misplayed ball.

Fake bunt. Assuming a bunting stance without attempting to hit the ball. Primarily used to draw basemen in close and away from their base-covering assignments.

Fair ball. A batted ball which is touched or stops in the infield between the foul lines, or which initially lands between the foul lines beyond the bases.

Fielder's choice. A play in which a fielder attempts to put out a runner, allowing another runner or runners to advance safely.

Force out. A putout on a baserunner who had to advance due to the batter becoming a baserunner.

Fungo. A self-tossed hit.

"Give" with the ball. To relax the arms, hands, and fingers as the ball enters the hands or glove.

Grounder. A batted ball on which no play is made before it hits or rolls on the ground.

Hit. A legally batted ball which results in the batter successfully getting on base through no error by the defensive team.

Hit-and-run. Offensive strategy in which the batter will hit and the baserunner will advance on the next pitch.

Hitting behind a runner. The act of place hitting the ball to an area of the field momentarily passed by an advancing baserunner.

Hop step (crow hop). Taking a short step on the throwing side foot and then a long step with the opposite foot.

Infield fly. A ball hit in the air into fair, infield territory which can be caught by an infielder. With less than two outs and baserunners on first or second, or first, second, and third, the infield fly rule is in effect.

Inning. A segment of the game in which each team is allowed three outs as the offensive team.

Interference. A hindrance by a player which prevents the opponent from making a play.

Lead-off. A quick move off the base taken by a baserunner as soon as the ball leaves the pitcher's hand (fast pitch).

Line drive. A batted ball hit on a plane parallel to the ground.

Obstruction. A defensive player, not involved in the play, interfering with the progress of an advancing baserunner.

Opposite field. Directing the ball to the field of the batter's dominant side, caused by swinging late. For a right-handed batter, the ball is hit to right field.

Opposite hand (side, foot, arm). The hand on the opposite side of the dominant or preferred hand.

Pickoff. An attempt to put out a player who has taken an extensive lead off a base.

Pitch out. A prearranged play in which the pitcher purposely throws high and to the outside of the plate when anticipating a stealing attempt by a runner on base.

Pivot person. The player, sometimes referred to as the middle person, who covers second base in a double play attempt.

Place hit. A batted ball which is intentionally hit to a specific area of the field.

Pulling the ball. Hitting for the field of the batter's non-dominant side. For a right-handed batter, directing the ball to left field by hitting early and following through.

Relay. An assisting throw by an infielder, or another outfielder when a long throw is necessary from an outfielder to the infield.

Rounding the bag. A curved advance toward the next base taken by a baserunner after safely passing a base.

Rundown. A defensive play designed to tag a baserunner trapped between two bases.

Sacrifice. A batted ball which intentionally advances a baserunner, but results in the batter being put out.

Shoestring catch. A ball caught just above the shoe tops or inches from the ground.

Short hop. Catching a ball just as it rebounds from the ground.

Squeeze bunt. A stealing attempt by a runner at third base as the batter bunts the pitch.

Stolen base. An advance from one base to another, credited to the baserunner, when no hit or walk has been made.

Straight away. Assuming a stance for hitting the ball through the central area of the diamond or field.

Strike zone. The area over the plate between the top of the batter's knees and the armpits (fast pitch) or shoulders (slow pitch).

Tag. Making a putout on an advancing baserunner by touching the player with the ball.

Tag up. On a fly ball hit to the outfield with less than two outs, the baserunner assumes a "get set" position on the base which permits a fast take off as the ball is caught or missed by the outfielder.

Texas leaguer. A looping ball hit between the infielders and the outfielders.

Throwing behind a runner. A misplayed attempt to put out a baserunner by throwing the ball to a base which the runner has passed.

Annotated Bibliography

General

Amateur Softball Association of America. *Softball: Official Rule Book and Guide, 1979*. Oklahoma City: Amateur Softball Association of America, 1979.

Incorporates both slow- and fast-pitch rules; provides data on national tournament results.

American Alliance for Health, Physical Education, and Recreation. *N.A.G.W.S. Softball Guide 1977-79*. Washington, D.C.: AAHPER, 1977.

Contains the official rules for both slow- and fast-pitch softball. Also includes articles on teaching fundamentals and strategy, information on officiating procedures, scoring, and rule adaptations.

American Alliance for Health, Physical Education, and Recreation. *Equipment and Supplies for Athletics, Physical Education and Recreation*. Washington, D.C.: AAHPER, 1960.

Offers an excellent section to assist the novice teacher or coach in ordering softball equipment. Includes quantitative guides in purchasing.

Bucher, Charles A.; Koenig, Constance P.; and Barnhard, Milton. *Methods and Materials for Secondary School Physical Education*, pp. 226-232, 313-314, 324-327, St. Louis: C. V. Mosby Company, 1970.

Thorough, detailed, and practical suggestions for organizing a group for instruction in a team sport.

Dobson, Margaret, and Sisley, Becky. *Softball for Girls*. New York: Ronald Press Company, 1971.

Includes explanation of fundamental skills, fielding responsibilities, offensive and defensive strategy, techniques of umpiring, information for setting up programs, and purchasing equipment. Excellent information of fast-pitch softball. Little is mentioned of the slow-pitch game and its rules and strategy.

Drysdale, Sharon, and Maley, Irene. "A Pre-season Softball Weight Training Program." *Softball Guide: January 1977-79*, p. 136. Washington, D.C.: AAHPER.

Suggests an excellent pre-season team conditioning program utilizing weight training and flexibility exercises.

Klafs, Carol, and Lyon, L. M. Joan. *The Female Athlete, Conditioning, Competition, and Culture*. St. Louis: C. V. Mosby, 1973.

Chapter 8 offers basic principles of conditioning and training appropriate in the development of male and female athletes. Includes information on weight training, isometric exercises, circuit training, and internal training.

Ledbetter, Virgil. *Coaching Baseball.* Dubuque, Iowa: William C. Brown Company, 1964.
Informative, thorough description of baseball techniques and strategy. Excellent sequential pictures of demonstrated skills.

National Federation of State High School Associations. *1980 Softball Rule Book.* Elgin, Illinois: National Federation of State High School Association, 1979.
Contains the rules and standards for interscholastic competition. Included are rule interpretations for various play situations.

Olson, Edward C. *Conditioning Fundamentals.* Columbus, Ohio: Charles E. Merrill, 1968.
Contains numerous exercises and weight workout programs classified according to the component of fitness developed by each.

Pennan, Kenneth. *Planning Physical Education and Athletic Facilities in Schools.* New York: John Wiley and Sons, 1977.
Describes the construction and layout of playing fields.

Wickstrom, Ralph L. *Fundamental Motor Patterns.* Philadelphia: Lea and Febiger, 1970.
Provides a detailed discussion of the movement patterns of six commonly used basic skills.

Skill Tests

Brace, David. *Skills Test Manual – Softball for Boys.* Washington, D.C.: AAHPER, 1966.
Describes eight skill tests developed by AAHPER. Tests are accompanied by procedures for their administration. To assist the physical educator in performance evaluation, national norms on male students 10 to 18 years of age are provided for each test.

Brace, David. *Skills Test Manual – Softball for Girls.* Washington D.C.: AAHPER, 1966.
Describes eight valid, softball skills tests with accompanying national norms on female students 10 to 18 years of age.

Shick, Jacqueline. "Battery of Defensive Softball Skills Tests" *Softball Guide: January 1972-74.* Washington D.C.: AAHPER, 1972.
Describes three softball skills tests designed to measure defensive abilities. Suitable as a motivational devise for college and secondary level players.

Drills and Lead-up Games

Blake, O., and Volp, Anne M. *Lead-up Games to Team Sports.* Englewood Cliffs, N.J.: Prentice-Hall, 1964.
A selection on softball presents several challenging lead-up games suitable for elementary or junior high school children. The games involve the fundamental skills of throwing, catching, batting, and baserunning.

Hoehn, Robert. "Six Man Slam. *The Coaching Clinic* 12 (1974):26.
Presents an interesting game-like drill incorporating hitting, fielding, and throwing the ball. Designed for baseball, but adaptable to softball practice for intermediate level players.

Knowles, Bobbie. "Softball Drills." Presented at the 1975 Florida Association for Health, Physical Education and Recreation Working Conference.
Provides selected drills which are appropriate for both slow- and fast-pitch softball classes and teams.

Littlewood, Mary. "Infield Action." *Coaching: Women's Athletics* 3 (1974):24.
Illustrates a multi-phased drill for infield practice. The suggested practice technique is designed to efficiently utilize practice time and promote maximal player involvement.

Lopiano, Donna. "Practice Schedule." *Coaching: Women's Athletics* 4 (1972):37.

Presents an effective station-to-station format for infield, outfield, and batting practice.

Russo, Joseph. "Developmental Drills for Outfielders." *The Coaching Clinic,* 14 (1976):10.

Presents four drills designed for practicing quick ball fielding. Drills are adaptable to intermediate or advanced level players.

Withers, Dan. "Indoor Circuit Training for Baseball, Part III." *The Coaching Clinic* 14 (1976):22.

Combines conditioning, ball handling, and bunting drills, organized in a station-to-station layout and suitable for practice in an indoor area. Good for team practices or an intermediate level class during inclement weather.

Visual Aids

Softball Film Loops

Softball. 12 super 8mm film loops of softball skills demonstrated by skilled women fast-pitch players. Suitable for secondary or post-secondary players and teachers. (Athletic Institute, 200 N. Castlewood Drive, North Palm Beach, FL 33408)

1. *Overhand Throw – Sidearm Throw*
2. *Catching above Waist – Catching below Waist*
3. *Fielding Long-Hit Fly Ball – Fielding Ground Balls*
4. *Batting*
5. *Sacrifice Bunt*
6. *Running to First Base – Running Extra Bases – Runner's Lead-off*
7. *Defensive Run Down*
8. *Hook Slide – Straight-in-Slide*
9. *Pitching – Windmill Style – Slingshot Style*
10. *Tag Outs – Force Outs*
11. *Double Play by Shortstop – Double Play by Second Basewomen*
12. *The Catcher*

Softball Series. Super 8mm. Color; sale $20 each.

Loops on batting, catching, fielding ground balls, pitching, and throwing. Appropriate technique instruction for elementary and junior high students. (BFA Education Media, 2211 Michigan Avenue, Santa Monica, CA 90406)

Filmstrips

Softball. Color. Filmstrips demonstrating the skills of the game, throwing, fielding, hitting, baserunning, pitching, base play and defense. (Athletic Institute, 705 Merchandise Mart, Chicago, IL 60654)

How to Improve Your Softball. For players, teachers and coaches (Amateur Softball Association of America, Oklahoma City, OK 73111)

Aids

Softball Technique Charts. Charts depicting the playing field, equipment and the skills of throwing, catching fielding, and batting. (AAHPER, 1201 16th Street N.W., Washington, D.C. 20036)

16mm Films

Baseball Fundamentals and Techniques. Sound; black and white; rental $16.50.

Instructional baseball. (Boston University Film Library, Boston, MA 02215)

Batting Fundamentals. Sound; black and white; rental $3.00.

Demonstrates stance, swing, follow through, and bunting. (Major League Baseball Film Division, 41 E. 42nd Street, New York, NY 10017)

Softball Fundamentals for Elementary Schools. Black and white; rental $3.50.

Fundamentals of throwing, catching, pitching, and safe play with young boys and girls demonstrating. (University of Southern California, Division of Cinema, Film Distribution, University Park, Los Angeles, CA 90007)

Softball . . . Playing It Right. Color; rental $2.00.

Techniques and differences of slow-pitch and fast-pitch as demonstrated by All-American players and championship teams. Excellent teaching aid. (Amateur Softball Association of America, 2801 N.E. 50th, Oklahoma City, OK 73111)

Softball: Skills and Practice. Color; rental $6.00; sale $150.

Demonstrates correct performance of each softball skill. Slow-motion photography provides opportunities for analyses. Good for elementary and junior and senior high students. (University of Southern California, Division of Cinema, Film Distribution, University Park, Los Angeles, CA 90007)

Softball Umpire Instructional Film. Sound; twenty minutes, color; free loan.

First softball film for umpires. Good for secondary or college level. (Amateur Softball Association of America, Oklahoma City, OK 73411)

Index